TANDEM

C000051654

Winston S. Churchill

The Roar of the Lion

It was Churchill himself who said, in one of his speeches, "Some people pretend to regard me as the British Lion. But I am not the Lion. I am simply the Roar of the Lion."

There is not a single word in this book which was not written or spoken by Churchill at one time or another. There are many volumes of his speeches available to the public and several of his written works, but here, for the first time in a single volume, is the essential Churchill, his life history in his own words arranged in chronological order, not of utterance, but of occurrence. The book begins with memories of himself as a schoolboy of eight and continues right through the battle of Sidney Street, the Battle of Britain, to the last days of his undying personality, so that it forms, in fact and with a flash of revelation, an autobiography from beyond the grave.

In these events, as he describes them himself, the man who may have been the last great Englishman strides back to life, massive, mountainous, monosyllabic, a master of the right word in the right place, a man towering above all others in humour, courage and the divine gift of leadership, a man who gave to his country hope, determination and, above all, *purpose*, a man who was, in very truth, the Roar of the Lion.

Winston S. Churchill

The Roar
of the Lion

TANDEM
33 Beauchamp Place, London, SW3

First published jointly in Great Britain by
Allan Wingate and Howard Baker Ltd
in Large Crown Octavo, 1969

This paperback edition first published in Great Britain by
Universal-Tandem Ltd 1969

Made and printed in Great Britain by
The Garden City Press Limited
Letchworth, Hertfordshire

The Publishers wish to record their
Acknowledgements and Thanks to
Messrs. Cassell & Co. Ltd., Eyre &
Spottiswoode Ltd. and the Paul Hamlyn
Group for permission to quote from their
published works of Sir Winston Churchill's
speeches and writings.
Publications by Messrs. Cassell & Co.
from which extracts have been included
in this volume are:

THE SECOND WORLD WAR	1948
EUROPE UNITE	1950
IN THE BALANCE	1951
STEMMING THE TIDE	1953
THE UNWRITTEN ALLIANCE	1961

"Some people pretend to regard me as The British Lion. But I am not The Lion. I am simply The Roar of the Lion."

WINSTON S. CHURCHILL

LIST OF ILLUSTRATIONS

between pages 128 and 129

Although always prepared for martyrdom, I preferred that it should be postponed.

My Early Life

It was at 'The Little Lodge' I was first menaced with Education. The approach of a sinister figure described as 'the Governess' was announced. Her arrival was fixed for a certain day. In order to prepare for this day Mrs. Everest produced a book called *Reading without Tears*. It certainly did not justify its title in my case. I was made aware that before the Governess arrived I must be able to read without tears. We toiled each day. My nurse pointed with a pen at the different letters. I thought it all very tiresome. Our preparations were by no means completed when the fateful hour struck and the Governess was due to arrive. I did what so many oppressed peoples have done in similar circumstances: I took to the woods. I hid in the extensive shrubberies —forests they seemed—which surrounded 'The Little Lodge'. Hours passed before I was retrieved and handed over to 'the Governess'.

My Early Life

My mother made the same brilliant impression upon my childhood's eye. She shone for me like the Evening Star. I loved her dearly—but at a distance. My nurse was my confidante. Mrs. Everest it was who looked after me and tended all my wants. It was to her I poured out my many troubles, both now and in my schooldays.

My Early Life

The school my parents had selected for my education was one of the most fashionable and expensive in the country. It modelled itself upon Eton and aimed at being preparatory for that Public School above all others. It was supposed to be the very last thing in schools. Only ten boys in a class; electric light (then a wonder); a swimming pond; spacious football and cricket grounds; two or three school treats, or 'expeditions' as they were called, every term; the masters all M.A.s in gowns and mortar-boards; a chapel of its own; no hampers allowed; everything provided by the authorities. It was a dark November afternoon when we arrived at this establishment. We had tea with the Headmaster, with whom my mother conversed in the most easy manner. I was pre-occupied with the fear of spilling my cup and so making 'a bad start'. I was also miserable at the idea of being left alone among all these strangers in this great, fierce, formidable place. After all I was only seven, and I had been so happy in my nursery with all my toys. I had such wonderful toys: a real steam engine, a magic lantern, and a collection of soldiers already nearly a thousand-strong. Now it was to be all lessons. Seven or eight hours of lessons every day except half-holidays, and football or cricket in addition.

When the last sound of my mother's departing wheels had died away, the Headmaster invited me to hand over any money I had in my possession. I produced my three halfcrowns, which were duly entered in a book, and I was told that from time to time there would be a 'shop' at the school with all sorts of things which one would like to have, and that I could choose what I liked up to the limit of seven and sixpence. Then we quitted the Headmaster's parlour and the comfortable private side of the house, and entered the more bleak apartments reserved for the instruction and accommodation of the pupils. I was taken into a Form Room and told to sit at a desk. All the other boys were out of doors, and I was alone with the Form Master. He produced a thin greeny-brown covered book filled with words in different types of print.

'You have never done any Latin before, have you?' he said.

'No, sir.'

'This is a Latin grammar.' He opened it at a well-thumbed page. 'You must learn this,' he said, pointing to a number of words in a frame of lines. 'I will come back in half an hour and see what you know.'

Behold me then on a gloomy evening, with an aching heart, seated in front of the First Declension.

Mensa	a table
Mensa	O table
Mensam	a table
Mensae	of a table
Mensae	to or for a table
Mensa	by, with or from a table

What on earth did it mean? Where was the sense in it? It seemed absolute rigmarole to me. However, there was one thing I could always do: I could learn by heart. And I thereupon proceeded, as far as my private sorrows would allow, to memorize the acrostic-looking task which had been set me.

In due course the Master returned.

'Have you learnt it?' he asked.

'I think I can say it, sir,' I replied; and I gabbled it off.

He seemed so satisfied with this that I was emboldened to ask a question.

'What does it mean, sir?'

'It means what it says. Mensa, a table. Mensa is a

noun of the First Declension. There are five declensions. You have learnt the singular of the First Declension.'

'But,' I repeated, 'what does it mean?'

'Mensa means a table,' he answered.

'Then why does mensa also mean O table,' I enquired, 'and what does O table mean?'

'Mensa, O table, is the vocative case,' he replied.

'But why O table?' I persisted in genuine curiosity.

'O table—you would use that in addressing a table, in invoking a table.' And then seeing he was not carrying me with him, 'You would use it in speaking to a table.'

'But I never do,' I blurted out in honest amazement.

'If you are impertinent, you will be punished, and punished, let me tell you, very severely,' was his conclusive rejoinder.

Such was my first introduction to the classics from which, I have been told, many of our cleverest men have derived so much solace and profit.

My Early Life

I had scarcely passed my twelfth birthday when I entered the inhospitable regions of examinations, through which for the next seven years I was destined to journey. These examinations were a great trial to me. The subjects which were dearest to the examiners were almost invariably those I fancied least. I would have liked to have been examined in history, poetry and writing essays. The examiners, on the other hand, were partial to Latin and mathematics. And their will prevailed. Moreover, the questions which they asked on both these subjects were almost invariably those to which I was unable to suggest a satisfactory answer. I should have liked to be asked to say what I knew. They always tried to ask what I did not know. When I would have willingly displayed my knowledge, they sought to expose my ignorance. This sort of treatment had only one result : I did not do well in examinations.

This was especially true of my Entrance Examination to Harrow. The Headmaster, Mr. Welldon, however, took a broad-minded view of my Latin prose : he showed discernment in judging my general ability. This was the more remarkable, because I was found unable to answer a single question in the Latin paper. I wrote my name at the top of the page. I wrote down the number of the question '1'. After much reflection I put a bracket round it thus '(1)'. But thereafter I could not think of anything connected with it that was either revelant or true. Incidentally, there arrived from nowhere in particular a blot and several smudges. I gazed for two whole hours at this sad spectacle : and then merciful ushers collected my piece of foolscap with all the others and carried it up to the Headmaster's table. It was from these slender indications of scholarship that Mr. Welldon drew the conclusion that I was worthy to pass into Harrow. It is very much to his credit. It showed that he was a man capable of looking beneath the surface of things : a man not dependent upon paper manifestations. I have always had the greatest regard for him.

I first went to Harrow in the summer term. The school possessed the biggest swimming-bath I had ever seen. It was more like the bend of a river than a bath, and it had two bridges across it. Thither we used to repair for hours at a time, and bask between our dips, eating enormous buns, on the hot asphalt margin. Naturally it was a good joke to come up behind some naked friend, or even enemy, and push him in. I made quite a habit of this with boys of my own size or less. One day when I had been no more than a month in the school, I saw a boy standing in a meditative posture wrapped in a towel on the very brink. He was no bigger than I was, so I thought him fair game. Coming stealthily behind, I pushed him in, holding on to his towel out of humanity so that it should not get wet. I was startled to see a furious face emerge from the foam, and a being evidently of enormous strength making its way by fierce strokes to the shore. I fled; but in vain. Swift as the wind my pursuer overtook me, seized me in a ferocious grip and hurled me into the deepest part of the pool. I soon scrambled out on the other side, and found myself surrounded by an agitated crowd of younger boys. 'You're for it,' they said. 'Do you know what you have done? It's Amery; he's in the Sixth Form. He is Head of his House; he is champion at Gym; he has got his football colours.' They continued to recount his many titles to fame and reverence, and to dilate upon the awful retribution that would fall upon me. I was convulsed not only with terror, but with the guilt of sacrilege. How could I tell his rank when he was in a bath-towel and so small? I determined to apologize immediately. I approached the potentate in lively trepidation. 'I am very sorry,' I said, 'I mistook you for a Fourth Form boy. You are so small.' He did not seem at all placated by this; so I added in a most brilliant recovery, 'My Father, who is a great man, is also small.' At this he laughed, and after some general remarks about my 'cheek' and how I had better be careful in the future, signified that the incident was closed. . . .

My Early Life

I do think unpunctuality is a vile habit, and all my life I have tried to break myself of it. 'I have never been able,' said Mr. Welldon to me some years later, 'to understand the point of view of persons who make a practice of being ten minutes late for each of a series of appointments throughout the day.' I entirely agree with

14

this dictum. The only straightforward course is to cut one or two of the appointments altogether and so catch up. But very few men have the strength of mind to do this. It is better that one notability should be turned away expostulating from the doorstep, than that nine just deputations should each fume for ten minutes in a stuffy ante-room.

My Early Life

I will here make some general observations about Latin which probably have their application to Greek as well. In a sensible language like English important words are connected and related to one another by other little words. The Romans in that stern antiquity considered such a method weak and unworthy. Nothing would satisfy them but that the structure of every word should be reacted on by its neighbours in accordance with elaborate rules to meet the different conditions in which it might be used. There is no doubt that this method both sounds and looks more impressive than our own. Then sentence fits together like a piece of polished machinery. Every phrase can be tensely charged with meaning. It must have been very laborious even if you were brought up to it; but no doubt it gave the Romans, and the Greeks too, a fine and easy way of establishing their posthumous fame. They were the first comers in the fields of thought and literature. When they arrived at fairly obvious reflections upon life and love, upon war, fate or manners, they coined them into the slogans or epigrams for which their language was so well adapted, and thus preserved the patent rights for all time. Hence their reputation. Nobody ever told me this at school. I have thought it all out in later life.

My Early Life

Horses were the greatest of my pleasures at Sandhurst. I and the group in which I moved spent all our money on hiring horses from the very excellent local livery stables. We ran up bills on the strength of our future commissions. We organized point-to-points and even a steeplechase in the park of a friendly grandee, and bucketed gaily about the countryside. And here I say to parents, and especially to wealthy parents, 'Don't give your son money. As far as you can afford it, give him horses.' No one ever came to grief—except honourable grief—through riding horses. No hour of life is lost that is spent in the saddle. Young men have often been ruined through owning horses, or through backing horses, but never through riding them; unless of course they break their necks, which taken at a gallop, is a very good death to die.

My Early Life

In my last term at Sandhurst—if the reader will permit a digression—my indignation was excited by the Purity Campaign of Mrs. Ormiston Chant. This lady was a member of the London County Council and in the summer of 1894 she started an active movement to purge our music-halls. Her attention was particularly directed to the promenade of the Empire Theatre. This large space behind the dress circle was frequently crowded during the evening performances, and especially on Saturdays, with young people of both sexes, who not only conversed together during the performance and its intervals, but also from time to time refreshed themselves with alcoholic liquors. Mrs. Ormiston Chant and her friends made a number of allegations affecting both the sobriety and the morals of these merrymakers; and she endeavoured to procure the closing of the promenade and above all of the bars which abutted on it. It seemed that the majority of the English public viewed these matters in a different light. Their cause was championed by the *Daily Telegraph*, in those days our leading popular newspaper. In a series of powerful articles headed 'Prudes on the Prowl' the *Daily Telegraph* inaugurated a wide and spirited correspondence to which persons were wont to contribute above such pseudonyms as 'Mother of Five', 'Gentleman and Christian', 'Live and Let Live', 'John Bull' and so forth. The controversy aroused keen public interest; but nowhere was it more searchingly debated than among my Sandhurst friends. We were accustomed to visit this very promenade in the brief leave allowed to us twice a month from Saturday noon till Sunday midnight. We were scandalized by Mrs. Chant's charges and insinuations. We had never seen anything to complain of in the behaviour of either sex. Indeed, the only point upon which criticism, as it seemed to us, might justly be directed was the strict and even rough manner in which the enormous uniformed commissionaires immediately removed, and even thrust forcibly into the street, anyone who had inadvertently overstepped the bounds of true temperance. We thought Mrs. Ormiston Chant's movement entirely uncalled for and contrary to the best traditions of British freedom.

In this cause I was keenly anxious to strike a blow. I noticed one day in the *Daily Telegraph* that a gentleman—whose name escapes me—proposed to found a League of Citizens to resist and counter the intolerance of Mrs. Chant and her backers. This was to be called 'The Entertainments Protection League'. The League proposed to form committees and an executive, to take offices and enrol members, to collect subscriptions, to hold public meetings, and to issue literature in support of its views. I immediately volunteered my services. I wrote to the pious Founder at the address which he had given, expressing my cordial agreement with his aims and my readiness to co-operate in every lawful way. In due course I received an answer on impressively-headed notepaper informing me that my support was welcomed, and inviting my attendance at the first meeting of the Executive Committee, which was to be held on the following Wednesday at 6 o'clock in a London hotel.

Wednesday was a half-holiday, and well-conducted cadets could obtain leave to go to London simply by asking for it. I occupied the three days' interval in composing a speech which I thought I might be called upon to deliver to a crowded executive of stern-faced citizens, about to unfurl that flag of British freedom for which 'Hampden died on the battlefield and Sidney on the scaffold'. As I had never attempted to speak in public before, it was a serious undertaking. I wrote and re-wrote my speech three or four times over, and committed it in all its perfection to my memory.

It was a serious constitutional argument upon the inherent rights of British usbjects; upon the dangers of State interference with the social habits of law-abiding persons; and upon the many evil consequences which inevitably follow upon repression not supported by healthy public opinion. It did not over-state the case, nor was it blind to facts. It sought to persuade by moderation and good humour, and to convince by logic tempered with common sense. There was even in its closing phases an appeal for a patient mood towards our misguided opponents. Was there not always more error than malice in human affairs? This task completed I awaited eagerly and at the same time nervously the momentous occasion.

As soon as our morning tasks were done I gobbled a hasty luncheon, changed into plain clothes (we were taught to abhor the word 'mufti', and such abominable

18

expressions as 'civvies' were in those days unknown) and hastened to the railway station, where I caught a very slow train to London. I must mention that this was for me a time of straitened finance; in fact the cost of the return railway ticket left me with only a few shillings in my pocket, and it was more than a fortnight before my next monthly allowance of £10 was due.

I whiled away the journey by rehearsing the points and passages on which I principally relied. I drove in a hansom cab from Waterloo to Leicester Square, near which the hotel appointed for the meeting of the Executive was situated. I was surprised and a little disconcerted at the dingy and even squalid appearance of these back streets and still more at the hotel when my cab eventually drew up before it. However, I said to myself they are probably quite right to avoid the fashionable quarters. If this movement is to prosper it must be based upon the people's will; it must respond to those simple instincts which all classes have in common. It must not be compromised by association with gilded youth or smart society. To the porter I said, 'I have come to attend the meeting of the Entertainments Protection League announced to be held this day in your hotel.'

The porter looked rather puzzled, and then said, 'I think there's a gentleman in the smoking-room about that.' Into the smoking-room, a small dark apartment, I was accordingly shown, and there I met face to face the Founder of the new body. He was alone. I was upset; but concealing my depression under the fast-vanishing rays of hope, I asked, 'When do we go up to the meeting?' He too seemed embarrassed. 'I have written to several people, but they have none of them turned up, so there's only you and me. We can draw up the Constitution ourselves, if you like.' I said, 'But you wrote to me on the headed paper of the League.' 'Well,' he said, 'that only cost 5s. It's always a good thing to have a printed heading on your notepaper in starting these sort of things. It encourages people to come forward. You see it encouraged you!' He paused as if chilled by my reserve, then added, 'It's very difficult to get people to do anything in England now. They take everything lying down. I do not know what's happened to the country; they seem to have no spirit left.'

Nothing was to be gained by carrying the matter further and less than nothing by getting angry with the Founder of the League. So I bade him a restrained but decisive farewell, and walked out into the street with a magnificent oration surging within my bosom and only half a crown in my pocket. The pavements were thronged with people hurrying to and fro engrossed upon their petty personal interests, oblivious and indifferent to the larger issues of human government. I looked with pity not untinged with scorn upon these trivial-minded passers-by. Evidently it was not going to be so easy to guide public opinion in the right direction as I had supposed. If these weak products of democracy held their liberties so lightly, how would they defend the vast provinces and domains we had gained by centuries of aristocratic and oligarchic rule? For a moment I despaired of the Empire. Then I thought of dinner and was pallidly confronted with the half a crown! No, that would not do! A journey to London on a beautiful half-holiday, keyed up to the last point of expectation, with a speech that might have shaped the national destinies undelivered and undigested upon my stomach, and then to go back to Sandhurst upon a bun and a cup of tea! That was more than fortitude could endure. So I did what I have never done before or since. I had now reached the Strand. I saw the three golden balls hanging over Mr. Attenborough's well-known shop. I had a very fine gold watch which my father had given me on my latest birthday. After all, the Crown Jewels of great kingdoms had been pawned on hard occasions. 'How much do you want?' said the shopman after handling the watch respectfully. 'A fiver will do,' I said. Some particulars were filled up in a book. I received one of those tickets which hitherto I had only heard of in music-hall songs, and a five-pound note, and sallied forth again into the heart of London. I got home all right.

The next day my Sandhurst friends all wanted to know how the meeting had gone off. I had imparted to them beforehand some of the more cogent arguments I intended to use. They were curious to learn how they had gone down. What was the meeting like? They had rather admired me for having the cheek to go up to make a speech championing their views to an Executive Committee of grown-up people, politicians, aldermen and the like. They wanted to know all about it. I did not admit them to my confidence. Speaking generally I dwelt upon the difficulties of public agitation in a comfortable and upon the whole contented country. I pointed out the importance of proceeding step by step, and of making each step good before the next was taken. The first step was to form an Executive Committee— that had been done. The next was to draw up the constitution of the League and assign the various responsibilities and powers—this was proceeding. The third step would be a broad appeal to the public, and on the response to this everything depended. These statements were accepted rather dubiously; but what else could I do? Had I only possessed a newspaper of my own, I would have had my speech reported verbatim on its front page, punctuated by the loud cheers of the Committee, heralded by arresting headlines and soberly sustained by the weight of successive leading articles. Then indeed the Entertainments Protection League might have made real progress. It might, in those early nineties, when so many things were in the making, have marshalled a public opinion so vigilant throughout the English-speaking world, and pronounced a warning so impressive, that the mighty United States themselves might have been saved from Prohibition! Here again we see the footprints of Fate, but they turned off the pleasant lawns on to a dry and stony highway.

I was destined to strike another blow in this crusade. Mrs. Chant's campaign was not unsuccessful, indeed so menacing did it appear that our party thought it prudent to make a characteristically British compromise. It was settled that the offending bars were to be separated from the promenade by light canvas screens. Thus they would no longer be technically 'in' the promenade; they would be just as far removed from it in law as if they had been in the adjacent county; yet means of egress and ingress of sufficient width might be lawfully provided, together with any reductions of the canvas screens necessary for efficient ventilation. Thus the temples of Venus and Bacchus, though adjacent, would be separated, and their attack upon human frailties could only be delivered in a successive or alternating and not in a concentrated form. Loud were the hosannas which arose from the steadfast ranks of the 'Prudes on the Prowl'. The music-hall proprietors for their part, after uttering howls of pain and protest, seemed to reconcile themselves quite readily to their lot. It was otherwise with the Sandhurst movement. We had not been consulted in this nefarious peace. I was myself filled with scorn at its hypocrisy. I had no idea in those days of the enormous and unquestionably helpful part that humbug plays in the social life of great peoples dwelling in a state of democratic freedom. I wanted a clear-cut definition of the duties of the state and of the rights of the individual, modified as might be necessary by public convenience and decorum.

On the first Saturday night after these canvas obstructions had been placed in the Empire promenade it happened that quite a large number of us chanced to be there. There were also a good many boys from the Universities about our own age, but of course mere bookworms, quite undisciplined and irresponsible. The new structures were examined with attention and soon became the subject of unfavourable comment. Then some young gentleman poked his walking-stick through the canvas. Others imitated his example. Naturally I could not hang back when colleagues were testifying after this fashion. Suddenly a most strange thing happened. The entire crowd numbering some two or three hundred people became excited and infuriated. They rushed upon these flimsy barricades and tore them to pieces. The authorities were powerless. Amid the cracking of timber and the tearing of canvas the barricades were demolished, and the bars were once more united with the promenade to which they had ministered so long.

In these somewhat unvirginal surroundings I now made my maiden speech. Mounting on the debris and indeed partially emerging from it, I addressed the tumultuous crowd. No very accurate report of my words has been preserved. They did not, however, fall unheeded, and I have heard about them several times since. I discarded the constitutional argument entirely and appealed directly to sentiment and even passion, finishing up by saying, 'You have seen us tear down these barricades to-night; see that you pull down those who are responsible for them at the coming election.' These words were received with rapturous applause, and we all sallied out into the Square brandishing fragments of wood and canvas as trophies or symbols. It reminded me of the death of Julius Caesar when the conspirators rushed forth into the street waving the bloody daggers with which they had slain the tyrant. I thought also of the taking of the Bastille, with the details of which I was equally familiar.

It seems even more difficult to carry forward a revolution than to start one. We had to catch the last train back to Sandhurst or be guilty of dereliction of duty. This train, which still starts from Waterloo shortly after midnight, conveys the daily toll of corpses to the London Necropolis. It ran only as far as Frimley near Aldershot which it reached at three o'clock in the morning, leaving us to drive eight or ten miles to the Royal Military College. On our arrival at this hamlet no conveyances were to be found. We therefore knocked up the local innkeeper. It may well be that we knocked him up rather boisterously. After a considerable interval in which our impatience became more manifest, the upper half of the door was suddenly opened, and we found ourselves looking down the muzzle of a blunderbuss, behind which stood a pale and menacing face. Things are rarely pushed to extremes in England. We maintained a firm posture, explained our wants and offered money. The landlord, first reassured and finally placated, produced an old horse and a still more ancient fly, and in this seven or eight of us made a successful journey to Camberley, and without troubling the porter at the gates, reached our apartments by unofficial paths in good time for early morning parade.

This episode made a considerable stir, and even secured leading articles in most of the newspapers. I was for some time apprehensive lest undue attention should be focused upon my share in the proceedings. Certainly there was grave risk, for my father's name was still electric. Although naturally proud of my part in resisting tyranny as is the duty of every citizen who wishes to live in a free country, I was not unaware that a contrary opinion was possible, and might even become predominant. Elderly people and those in authority cannot always be relied upon to take enlightened and comprehending views of what they call the indiscretions of youth. They sometimes have a nasty trick of singling out individuals and 'making examples'. Although always prepared for martyrdom, I preferred that it should be postponed. Happily by the time my name began to be connected with the event, public interest had entirely died down, and no one at the College or the War Office was so spiteful as to revive it. This was one of those pieces of good luck which ought always to be remembered to set against an equal amount of bad luck when it comes along, as come it must. It remains only for me to record that the County Council Elections went the wrong way. The Progressives, as they called themselves, triumphed. The barracades were rebuilt in brick and plaster, and all our efforts went for nothing. Still no one can say we did not do our best.

My Early Life

I have no doubt that the Romans planned the time-table of their days far better than we do. They rose before the sun at all seasons. Except in wartime we never see the dawn. Sometimes we see sunset. The message of the sunset is sadness : the message of the dawn is hope. The rest and the spell of sleep in the middle of the day refresh the human frame far more than a long night. We were not made by Nature to work, or even

25

to play, from eight o'clock in the morning till midnight. We throw a strain upon our system which is unfair and improvident. For every purpose of business or pleasure, mental or physical, we ought to break our days and our marches into two. When I was at the Admiralty in the War, I found I could add nearly two hours to my working effort by going to bed for an hour after luncheon. The Latins are wiser and closer to Nature in their way of living than the Anglo-Saxons or Teutons. But they dwell in superior climates.

My Early Life

It is hard, if not impossible, to snub a beautiful woman —they [sic] remain beautiful and the rebuke recoils.

Savrola

It often happens that, when men are convinced that they have to die, a desire to bear themselves well and to leave Life's stage with dignity conquers all other sensations.

Savrola 1900

It was not until this winter of 1896, when I had almost completed my twenty-second year, that the desire for learning came upon me. I began to feel myself wanting in even the vaguest knowledge about many large spheres of thought. I had picked up a wide vocabulary and had a liking for words and for the feel of words fitting and falling into their places like pennies in the slot. I caught myself using a good many words the meaning of which I could not define precisely. I admired these words, but was afraid to use them for fear of being absurd. One day, before I left England, a friend of mine had said: 'Christ's gospel was the last word in Ethics.' This sounded good; but what were

Ethics? They had never been mentioned to me at Harrow or Sandhurst. Judging from the context I thought they must mean 'the public school spirit', 'playing the game', 'esprit de corps', 'honourable behaviour', 'patriotism', and the like. Then someone told me that Ethics were concerned not merely with the things you ought to do, but with why you ought to do them, and that there were whole books written on the subject. I would have paid some scholar £2 at least to give me a lecture of an hour or an hour and a half about Ethics. What was the scope of the subject; what were its main branches; what were the principal questions dealt with, and the chief controversies open; who were the high authorities and which were the standard books? But here in Bangalore there was no one to tell me about Ethics for love or money. Of tactics I had a grip: on politics I had a view: but a concise compendious outline of Ethics was a novelty not to be locally obtained.

Then someone had used the phrase 'the Socratic method'. What was that? It was apparently a way of giving your friend his head in an argument and progging him into a pity by cunning questions. Who was Socrates, anyhow? A very argumentative Greek who had a nagging wife and was finally compelled to commit suicide because he was a nuisance! Still, he was beyond doubt a considerable person. He counted for a lot in the minds of learned people. I wanted 'the Socrates story'. Why had his fame lasted through all the ages? What were the stresses which had led a government to put him to death merely because of the things he said? Dire stresses they must have been: the life of the Athenian Executive or the life of this talkative professor! Such antagonisms do not spring from petty issues. Evidently Socrates had called something into being long ago which was very explosive. Intellectual dynamite! A moral bomb! But there was nothing about it in The Queen's Regulations.

Then there was history. I had always liked history at school. But there we were given only the dullest, driest pemmicanized forms like *The Student's Hume*. Once I had a hundred pages of *The Student's Hume* as a holiday task. Quite unexpectedly, before I went back to school, my father set out to examine me upon it. The period was Charles I. He asked me about the Grand Remonstrance; what did I know about that? I said that in the end the Parliament beat the King and cut his head off. This seemed to me the grandest remonstrance imaginable. It was no good. 'Here,' said my father, 'is a grave parliamentary question affecting the whole structure of our constitutional history, lying near the centre of the task you have been set, and you do not in the slightest degree appreciate the issues involved.' I was puzzled by his concern : I could not see at the time why it should matter so much. Now I wanted to know more about it.

So I resolved to read history, philosophy, economics, and things like that; and I wrote to my mother asking for such books as I had heard of on these topics. She responded with alacrity, and every month the mail brought me a substantial package of what I thought were standard works. In history I decided to begin with Gibbon. Someone had told me that my father had read Gibbon with delight; that he knew whole pages of it by heart, and that it had greatly affected his style of speech and writing. So without more ado I set out upon the eight volumes of Dean Milman's edition of Gibbon's *Decline and Fall of the Roman Empire*. I was immediately dominated both by the story and the style. All through the long glistening middle hours of the Indian day, from when we quitted stables till the evening shadows proclaimed the hour of Polo, I devoured Gibbon. I rode triumphantly through it from end to end and enjoyed it all. I scribbled all my opinions on the margins of the pages, and very soon found myself a vehement partisan of the author against the disparagments of his pompous-pious editor. I was not even estranged by his naughty footnotes. On the other hand the Dean's apologies and disclaimers roused my ire. So pleased was I with *The Decline and Fall* that I began at once to read Gibbon's *Autobiography,* which luckily was bound up in the same edition. When I read his reference to his old nurse: 'If there be any, as I trust there are some, who rejoice that I live, to that dear and excellent woman their gratitude is due', I thought of Mrs. Everest; and it shall be her epitaph.

From Gibbon I went to Macaulay. I had learnt *The Lays of Ancient Rome* by heart, and loved them; and of course I knew he had written a history; but I had never read a page of it. I now embarked on that splendid romance. And I voyaged with full sail in a strong wind. I remembered then that Mrs. Everest's brother-in-law, the old prison warder, had possessed a copy of Macaulay's *History,* purchased in supplements and bound together, and that he used to speak of it with reverence. I accepted all Macaulay wrote as gospel, and I was grieved to read his harsh judgments upon the great Duke of Marlborough. There was no one at hand to tell me that this historian with his captivating style and devastating self-confidence was the prince of literary rogues, who always preferred the tale to the truth, and smirched or glorified great men and garbled documents according as they affected his drama. I cannot forgive him for imposing on my confidence and on the simple faith of my old friend the warder. Still I must admit an immense debt upon the other side.

From November to May I read for four or five hours

every day history and philosophy. Plato's *Republic*—it appeared he was for all practical purposes the same as Socrates; the *Politics of Aristotle,* edited by Mr. Welldon himself; *Schopenhauer on Pessimism*; *Malthus on Population;* Darwin's *Origin of Species* : all interspersed with other books of lesser standing. It was a curious education. First because I approached it with an empty, hungry mind, and with fairly strong jaws; and what I got I bit; secondly because I had no one to tell me : 'This is discredited.' 'You should read the answer to that by so and so; the two together will give you the gist of the argument.' 'There is a much better book on that subject', and so forth. I now began for the first time to envy those young cubs at the university who had fine scholars to tell them what was what; professors who had devoted their lives to mastering and focusing ideas in every branch of learning; who were eager to distribute the treasures they had gathered before they were overtaken by the night. But now I pity undergraduates, when I see what frivolous lives many of them lead in the midst of precious fleeting opportunity. After all, a man's Life must be nailed to a cross either of Thought or Action. Without work there is no play.

When I am in the Socratic mood and planning my Republic, I make drastic changes in the education of the sons of well-to-do citizens. When they are sixteen or seventeen they begin to learn a craft and to do healthy manual labour, with plenty of poetry, songs, dancing, drill and gymnastics in their spare time. They can thus let off their steam on something useful. It is only when they are really thirsty for knowledge, longing to hear about things, that I would let them go to the University. It would be a favour, a coveted privilege, only to be given to those who had either proved their worth in factory or field or whose qualities and zeal were preeminent. However, this would upset a lot of things; it would cause commotion and bring me perhaps in the end a hemlock draught.

My various readings during the next two years led me to ask myself questions about religion. Hitherto I had dutifully accepted everything I had been told. Even in the holidays I always had to go once a week to church, and at Harrow there were three services every Sunday, besides morning and evening prayers throughout the week. All this was very good. I accumulated in those years so fine a surplus in the Bank of Observance that I have been drawing confidently upon it ever since. Weddings, christenings, and funerals have brought in a steady annual income, and I have never made too close enquiries about the state of my account. It might well even be that I should find an overdraft. But now in these bright days of youth my attendances were well ahead of the Sundays. In the Army too there were regular church parades, and sometimes I marched the Roman Catholics to church, and sometimes the Protestants. Religious toleration in the British Army had spread until it overlapped the regions of indifference. No one was ever hampered or prejudiced on account of his religion. Everyone had the regulation facilities for its observance. In India the deities of a hundred creeds were placed by respectful routine in the Imperial Pantheon. In the regiment we sometimes used to argue questions like 'Whether we should live again in another world after this was over?' 'Whether we have ever lived before?' 'Whether we remember and meet each other after Death or merely start again like the Buddhists?' 'Whether some high intelligence is looking after the world or whether things are just drifting on anyhow?' There was general agreement that if you tried your best to live an honourable life and did your duty and were faithful to friends and not unkind to the weak and poor, it did not matter much what you believed or disbelieved. All would come out right. This is what would nowadays I suppose be called 'The Religion of Healthy-Mindedness'.

As it was I passed through a violent and aggressive anti-religious phase which, had it lasted, might easily have made me a nuisance. My poise was restored during the next few years by frequent contact with danger. I found that whatever I might think and argue, I did not hesitate to ask for special protection when about to come under the fire of the enemy : nor to feel sincerely grateful when I got home safe to tea. I even asked for lesser things than not to be killed too soon, and nearly always in these years, and indeed throughout my life, I got what I wanted. This practice seemed perfectly natural, and just as strong and real as the reasoning process which contradicted it so sharply. Moreover the practice was comforting and the reasoning led nowhere. I therefore acted in accordance with my feelings without troubling to square such conduct with the conclusions of thought.

It is a good thing for an uneducated man to read books of quotations. Bartlett's *Familiar Quotations* is an admirable work, and I studied it intently. The quotations when engraved upon the memory give you good thoughts. They also make you anxious to read the authors and look for more. In this or some other similar book I came across a French saying which seemed singularly apposite. 'Le coeur a ses raisons, que la raison ne connait pas.' It seemed to me that it would be very foolish to discard the reasons of the heart for those of the head. Indeed I could not see why I should not enjoy them both. I did not worry about the inconsistency of thinking one way and believing the other. It seemed

32

good to let the mind explore so far as it could the paths of thought and logic, and also good to pray for help and succour, and be thankful when they came. I could not feel that the Supreme Creator who gave us our minds as well as our souls would be offended if they did not always run smoothly together in double harness. After all He must have foreseen this from the beginning and of course He would understand it all.

Accordingly I have always been surprised to see some of our Bishops and clergy making such heavy weather about reconciling the Bible story with modern scientific and historical knowledge. Why do they want to reconcile them? If you are the recipient of a message which cheers your heart and fortifies your soul, which promises you reunion with those you have loved in a world of larger opportunity and wider sympathies, why should you worry about the shape or colour of the travel-stained envelope; whether it is duly stamped, whether the date on the postmark is right or wrong? These matters may be puzzling, but they are certainly not important. What is important is the message and the benefits to you of receiving it. Close reasoning can conduct one to the precise conclusion that miracles are impossible : that 'it is much more likely that human testimony should err, than that the laws of nature should be violated'; and at the same time one may rejoice to read how Christ turned the water into wine in Cana of Galilee or walked on the lake or rose from the dead. The human brain cannot comprehend infinity, but the discovery of mathematics enables it to be handled quite easily. The idea that nothing is true except what we comprehend is silly, and that ideas which our minds cannot reconcile are mutually destructive, sillier still. Certainly nothing could be more repulsive both to our minds and feelings than the spectacle of thousands of millions of universes—for

33

that is what they say it comes to now—all knocking about together for ever without any rational or good purpose behind them. I therefore adopted quite early in life a system of believing whatever I wanted to believe, while at the same time leaving reason to pursue unfettered whatever paths she was capable of treading.

Some of my cousins who had the great advantage of University education used to tease me with arguments to prove that nothing has any existence except what we think of it. The whole creation is but a dream; all phenomena are imaginary. You create your own universe as you go along. The stronger your imagination, the more variegated your universe. When you leave off dreaming, the universe ceases to exist. These amusing mental acrobatics are all right to play with. They are perfectly harmless and perfectly useless. I warn my younger readers only to treat them as a game. The metaphysicians will have the last word and defy you to disprove their absurd propositions.

I always rested upon the following argument which I devised for myself many years ago. We look up in the sky and see the sun. Our eyes are dazzled and our senses record the fact. So here is this great sun standing apparently on no better foundation than our physical senses. But happily there is a method, apart altogether from our physical senses, of testing the reality of the sun. It is by mathematics. By means of prolonged processes of mathematics, entirely separate from the senses, astronomers are able to calculate when an eclipse will occur. They predict by pure reason that a black spot will pass across the sun on a certain day. You go and look, and your sense of sight immediately tells you that their calculations are vindicted. So here you have the evidence of the senses reinforced by the entirely separate evidence of a vast independent process of mathematical reasoning. We have taken what is called in military map-making a 'cross-bearing'. We have got independent testimony to the reality of the sun. When my metaphysical friends tell me that the data on which the astronomers made their calculations, were necessarily obtained originally through the evidence of the senses, I say 'No'. They might, in theory, at any rate, be obtained by automatic calculating-machines set in motion by the light falling upon them without admixture of the human senses at any stage. When it is persisted that we should have to be told about the calculations and use our ears for that purpose, I reply that the mathematical process has a reality and virtue in itself, and that once discovered it constitutes a new and independent factor. I am also at this point accustomed to reaffirm with emphasis my conviction that the sun is real, and also that it is hot—in fact as hot as Hell, and that if the metaphysicians doubt it they should go there and see.

My Early Life

I have noticed in the last three wars in which we have been engaged a tendency among military officers—arising partly from good nature towards their comrades, partly from dislike of public scrutiny—to hush everything up, to make everything look as fair as possible, to tell what is called the official truth, to present a version of truth which contains about seventy-five per cent of the actual article. So long as a force gets a victory somehow, all the ugly facts are smoothed and varnished over, rotten reputations are propped up, and officers known as incapable are allowed to hang on and linger in their commands in the hope that at the end of the war they may be shunted into private life without a scandal.

Commons, March 12, 1901

A European war can end only in the ruin of the vanquished and the scarcely less fatal commercial dislocation and exhaustion of the conquerors. Democracy is more vindictive than cabinets. The wars of peoples will be more terrible than those of kings.

Commons, May 12, 1901

A blunderbuss is a traditional weapon with which the British householded defends himself from those who seek to plunder him.

Commons, May 13, 1901

. . . I decided to go with the second party up the long spur towards the village. I gave my pony to a native and began to toil up the hillside with the infantry. It was frightfully hot. The sun, nearing the meridian, beat upon one's shoulders. We plodded and stumbled upwards for nearly an hour—now through high patches of Indian corn, now over boulders, now along stony tracks or over bare slopes—but always mounting. A few shots were fired from higher up the mountain; but otherwise complete peace seemed to reign. As we ascended, the whole oval pan of the Mamund Valley spread out behind us, and pausing to mop my brow, I sat on a rock and surveyed it. It was already nearly eleven o'clock. The first thing that struck me was that there were no troops to be seen. About half a mile from the foot of the spur a few of the Lancers were dismounted. Far off against the distant mountain wall a thin column of smoke rose from a burning castle. Where was our Army? They had marched out twelve hundred strong only a few hours ago, and now the valley had swallowed them all up. I took out my glasses and searched the plain. Mud villages and castles here and there, the deep-cut watercourses, the gleam of reservoirs, occasional belts of

cultivation, isolated groves of trees—all in a
atmosphere backed by serrated cliffs—but of a
Indian brigade, no sign.

It occurred to me for the first time that we
very small party; five British officers including myself,
and probably eighty-five Sikhs. That was absolutely all;
and here we were at the very head of the redoubtable
Mamund Valley, scrambling up to punish its farthest
village. I was fresh enough from Sandhurst to remember
the warnings about 'dispersion of forces', and certainly
it seemed that the contrast between precautions which
our strong force had taken moving out of camp in the
morning, and the present position of our handful of
men, was remarkable. However, like most young fools I
was looking for trouble, and only hoped that something
exciting would happen. It did!

At last we reached the few mud houses of the village.
Like all the others, it was deserted. It stood at the head
of the spur, and was linked to the mass of the mountains
by a broad neck. I lay down with an officer and eight
Sikhs on the side of the village towards the mountain,
while the remainder of the company rummaged about
the mud houses or sat down and rested behind them. A
quarter of an hour passed and nothing happened. Then
the Captain of the company arrived.

'We are going to withdraw,' he said to the subaltern.
'You stay here and cover our retirement till we take up
a fresh position on that knoll below the village.' He
added, 'The Buffs don't seem to be coming up, and the
Colonel thinks we are rather in the air here.'

It struck me this was a sound observation. We waited
another ten minutes. Meanwhile I presumed, for I
could not see them, the main body of the company was
retiring from the village towards the lower knoll. Suddenly the mountain-side sprang to life. Swords flashed

37

rom behind rocks, bright flags waved here and there. A dozen widely-scattered white smoke-puffs broke from the rugged face in front of us. Loud explosions resounded close at hand. From high up on the crag, one thousand, two thousand, three thousand feet above us, white or blue figures appeared, dropping down the mountain-side from ledge to ledge like monkeys down the branches of a tall tree. A shrill crying arose from many points. Yi! Yi! Yi! Bang! Bang! Bang! The whole hillside began to be spotted with smoke, and tiny figures descended every moment nearer towards us. Our eight Sikhs opened an independent fire, which soon became more and more rapid. The hostile figures continued to flow down the mountain-side, and scores began to gather in rocks about a hundred yards away from us. The targets were too tempting to be resisted. I borrowed the Martini of the Sikh by whom I lay. He was quite content to hand me cartridges. I began to shoot carefully at the men gathering in the rocks. A lot of bullets whistled about us. But we lay very flat, and no harm was done. This lasted perhaps five minutes in continuous crescendo. We had certainly found the adventure for which we had been looking. Then an English voice close behind. It was the Battalion Adjutant.

'Come on back now. There is no time to lose. We can cover you from the knoll.'

The Sikh whose rifle I had borrowed had put eight or ten cartridges on the ground beside me. It was a standing rule to let no ammunition fall into the hands of the tribesmen. The Sikh seemed rather excited, so I handed him the cartridges one after the other to put in his pouch. This was a lucky inspiration. The rest of our party got up and turned to retreat. There was a ragged volley from the rocks; shouts, exclamations, and a scream. I thought for the moment that five or six of our men had lain down again. So they had: two killed and three wounded. One man was shot through the breast and pouring with blood; another lay on his back kicking and twisting. The British officer was spinning round just behind me, his face a mass of blood, his right eye cut out. Yes, it was certainly an adventure.

It is a point of honour on the Indian frontier not to leave wounded men behind. Death by inches and hideous mutilation are the invariable measure meted out to all who fall in battle into the hands of the Pathan tribesmen. Back came the Adjutant, with another British officer of subaltern rank, a Sikh sergeant-major, and two or three soldiers. We all laid hands on the wounded and began to carry and drag them away down the hill. We got through the few houses, ten or twelve men carrying four, and emerged upon a bare strip of ground. Here stood the Captain commanding the company with half a dozen men. Beyond and below, one hundred and fifty yards away, was the knoll on which a supporting party should have been posted. No sign of them! Perhaps it was the knoll lower down. We hustled the wounded along, regardless of their protests. We had no rearguard of any kind. All were carrying the wounded. I was therefore sure that worse was close at our heels. We were not half-way across the open space when twenty or thirty furious figures appeared among the houses, firing frantically or waving their swords.

I could only follow by fragments what happened after that. One of the two Sikhs helping to carry my wounded man was shot through the calf. He shouted with pain; his turban fell off; and his long black hair streamed over his shoulders—a tragic golliwog. Two more men came from below and seized hold of our man. The new subaltern and I got the golliwog by the collar and dragged him along the ground. Luckily it was all downhill. Apparently we hurt him so much on the sharp rocks that he asked to be let go of. He hopped and crawled and staggered and stumbled, but made a good pace. Thus he escaped. I looked round to my left. The Adjutant had been shot. Four of his soldiers were carrying him. He was a heavy man, and they all clutched at him. Out from the edge of the houses rushed half a dozen Pathan swordsmen. The bearers of the poor Adjutant let him fall and fled at their approach. The leading tribesman rushed upon the prostrate figure and slashed it three or four times with his sword. I forgot everything else at this moment except a desire to kill this man. I wore my long cavalry sword well sharpened. After all, I had won the Public Schools fencing medal. I resolved on personal combat a l'arme blanche. The savage saw me coming. I was not more than twenty yards away. He picked up a big stone and hurled it at me with his left hand, and then awaited me, brandishing his sword. There were others waiting not far behind him. I changed my mind about the cold steel. I pulled out my revolver, took, as I thought, most careful aim, and fired. No result. I fired again. No result. I fired again. Whether I hit him or not I cannot tell. At any rate he ran back two or three yards and plumped down behind a rock. The fusilade was continuous. I looked around. I was all alone with the enemy. Not a friend to be seen. I ran as fast as I could. There were bullets everywhere. I got to the first knoll. Hurrah, there were the Sikhs holding the lower one! They made vehement gestures, and in a few moments I was among them.

My Early Life

It is always, I think, true to say that one of the main foundations of the British sense of humour is understatement.

Nothing can save England if she will not save herself. If we lose faith in ourselves, in our capacity to guide and govern, if we lose our will to live, then indeed our story is told.

RANGE. The British Empire has been built up by running risks. If we had never moved an inch beyond the range of our heavy artillery, our empire would probably have been limited by that same scope.

POMP AND POWER. On the whole it is wise in human affairs, and in the government of men, to separate pomp from power.

THE BATTLE OF OMDURMAN

The bugles all over the camp by the river began to sound at half past four. The cavalry trumpets and the drums and fifes of the British division joined the chorus, and everyone awoke amid a confusion of merry or defiant notes. Then it grew gradually lighter, and the cavalry mounted their horses, the infantry stood to their arms, and the gunners went to their batteries; while the sun, rising over the Nile, revealed the wide plain, the dark rocky hills, and the waiting army. It was as if all the preliminaries were settled, the ground cleared, and nothing remained but the final act and 'the rigour of the game'.

Even before it became light several squadrons of British and Egyptian cavalry were pushed swiftly forward to gain contact with the enemy and learn his intentions. The first of these, under Captain Baring, occupied Surgham Hill, and waited in the gloom until the whereabouts of the Dervishes should be disclosed by the dawn. It was a perilous undertaking, for he might have found them unexpectedly near. As the sun rose, the 21st Lancers trotted out of the zeriba and threw out a spray of officers' patrols. As there had been no night attack, it was expected that the Dervish army would have retired to their original position or entered the town. It was hardly conceivable that they would advance across the open ground to attack the zeriba by daylight. Indeed, it appeared more probable that their hearts had failed them in the night, and that they had melted away into the desert. But these anticipations were immediately dispelled by the scene which was visible from the crest of the ridge.

It was a quarter to six. The light was dim, but growing stronger every minute. There in the plain lay the enemy, their numbers unaltered, their confidence and intentions apparently unshaken. Their front was now nearly five miles long, and composed of great masses of men joined together by thinner lines. Behind and near to the flanks were large reserves. From the ridge they looked dark blurs and streaks, relieved and diversified with an odd-looking shimmer of light from the spear-points. At about ten minutes to six it was evident that the masses were in motion and advancing swiftly. Their Emirs galloped about and before their ranks. Scouts and patrols scattered themselves all over the front. Then they began to cheer. They were still a mile away from the hill, and were concealed from the Sirdar's army by the folds of the ground. The noise of the shouting was heard, albeit faintly, by the troops down by the river. But to those watching on the hill a tremendous roar came up in waves of intense sound, like the tumult of the rising wind and sea before a storm.

The British and Egyptian forces were arranged in line,

with their back to the river. The flanks were secured by the gunboats lying moored in the stream. Before them was the rolling sandy plain, looking from the slight elevation of the ridge smooth and flat as a table. To the right rose the rocky hills of the Kerreri position, near which the Egyptian cavalry were drawn up—a dark solid mass of men and horses. On the left the 21st Lancers, with a single squadron thrown out in advance, were halted watching their patrols, who climbed about Surgham Hill, stretched forward beyond it, or perched, as we did, on the ridge.

The ground sloped gently up from the river, so that it seemed as if the landward ends of the Surgham and Kerreri ridges curved in towards each other, enclosing what lay between. Beyond the long swell of sand which formed the western wall of this spacious amphitheatre the black shapes of the distant hills rose in misty confusion. The challengers were already in the arena; their antagonists swiftly approached.

Although the Dervishes were steadily advancing, a belief that their musketry was inferior encouraged a nearer view, and we trotted round the south-west slopes of Surgham Hill until we reached the sandhills on the enemy's side, among which the regiment had waited the day before. Thence the whole array was visible in minute detail. It seemed that every single man of all the thousands could be examined separately. The pace of their march was fast and steady and it was evident that it would not be safe to wait long among the sandhills. Yet the wonder of the scene exercised a dangerous fascination, and for a while we tarried.

The emblems of the more famous Emirs were easily distinguishable. On the extreme left the chiefs and soldiers of the bright green flag gathered under Ali-Wad-Helu; between this and the centre the large dark green flag of Osman Sheikh-ed-Din rose above a dense mass of spearmen, preceded by long lines of warriors armed presumably with rifles; over the centre, commanded by Yakub, the sacred Black banner of the Khalifa floated high and remarkable; while on the right a great square of Dervishes was arrayed under an extraordinary number of white flags, amid which the red ensign of Sherif was almost hidden. All the pride and might of the Dervish Empire were massed on this last great day of its existence. Riflemen who had helped to destroy Hicks, spearmen who had charged at Abu Klea, Emirs who saw the sack of Gondar, Baggara fresh from raiding the Shillooks, warriors who had besieged Khartoum—all marched, inspired by the memories of former triumphs and embittered by the knowledge of late defeats, to chastise the impudent and accursed invaders.

The advance continued. The Dervish left began to stretch out across the plain towards Kerreri—as I thought, to turn our right flank. Their centre, under the Black Flag, moved directly towards Surgham. The right pursued a line of advance south of that hill. This mass of men were the most striking of all. They could not have mustered fewer than 6,000. Their array was perfect. They displayed a great number of flags—perhaps 500—which looked at the distance white, though they were really covered with texts from the Koran, and which by their admirable alignment made this division of the Khalifa's army look like the old representations of the Crusaders in the Bayeux tapestry. . . .

The Dervish centre had come within range. But it was not the British and Egyptian army that began the battle. If there was one arm in which the Arabs were beyond all comparison inferior to their adversaries, it was in guns. Yet it was with this arm that they opened their attack. In the middle of the Dervish line now

44

marching in frontal assault were two puffs of smoke. About fifty yards short of the thorn fence two red clouds of sand and dust sprang up, where the projectiles had struck. It looked like a challenge. It was immediately answered. Great clouds of smoke appeared all along the front of the British and Soudanese brigades. One after another four batteries opened on the enemy at a range of about 3,000 yards. The sound of the cannonade rolled up to us on the ridge, and was re-echoed by the hills. Above the heads of the moving masses shells began to burst, dotting the air with smoke-balls and the ground with bodies. But a nearer tragedy impended. The 'White Flags' were nearly over the crest. In another minute they would become visible to the batteries. Did they realize what would come to meet them? They were in a dense mass, 2,800 yards from the 32nd Field Battery and the gunboats. The ranges were known. It was a matter of machinery. The more distant slaughter passed unnoticed, as the mind was fascinated by the approaching horror. In a few seconds swift destruction would rush on these brave men. They topped the crest and drew out into full view of the whole army. Their white banners made them conspicuous above all. As they saw the camp of their enemies, they discharged their rifles with a great roar of musketry and quickened their pace. For a moment the white flags advanced in regular order, and the whole division crossed the crest and were exposed. Forthwith the gunboats, the 32nd British Field Battery, and other guns from the zeriba opened on them. About twenty shells struck them in the first minute. Some burst high in the air, others exactly in their faces. Others, again, plunged into the sand, exploding, dashed clouds of red dust, splinters, and bullets amid their ranks. The white banners toppled over in all directions. Yet they rose again immediately, as other men pressed forward

45

to die for the Madhi's sacred cause and in the defence of the successor of the True Prophet. It was a terrible sight, for as yet they had not hurt us at all, and it seemed an unfair advantage to strike thus cruelly when they could not reply. Under the influence of the shells the mass of the 'White Flags' dissolved into thin lines of spearmen and skirmishers, and came on in altered formation and diminished numbers, but with unabated enthusiasm. And now, the whole attack being thoroughly exposed, it became the duty of the cavalry to clear the front as quickly as possible, and leave the further conduct of the debate to the infantry and the Maxim guns. All the patrols trotted or cantered back to their squadrons, and the regiment retired swiftly into the zeriba, while the shells from the gunboats screamed overhead and the whole length of the position began to burst into flame and smoke. Nor was it long before the tremendous banging of the artillery was swollen by the roar of musketry.

Eight hundred yards away a ragged line of men were coming on desperately, struggling forward in the face of the pitiless fire—white banners tossing and collapsing; white figures subsiding in dozens to the ground; little white puffs from their rifles, larger white puffs spreading in a row all along their front from the bursting shrapnel.

The infantry fired steadily and stolidly, without hurry or excitement, for the enemy were far away and the officers careful. Besides, the soldiers were interested in the work and took great pains. But presently the mere physical act became tedious. The tiny figures seen over the slide of the back-sight seemed a little larger, but also fewer at each successive volley. The rifles grew hot —so hot that they had to be changed for those of the reserve companies. The Maxim guns exhausted all the water in their jackets, and several had to be refreshed from the water-bottles of the Cameron Highlanders before they could go on with their deadly work. The empty cartridge-cases, tinkling to the ground, formed a small but growing heat beside each man. And all the time out on the plain on the other side bullets were shearing through flesh, smashing and splintering bone; blood spouted from terrible wounds; valiant men were struggling on through a hell of whistling metal; exploding shells, and spurting dust—suffering, despairing, dying. Such was the first phase of the battle of Omdurman.

As the 21st Lancers left the ridge, the fire of the Arab riflemen on the hill ceased. We advanced at a walk in mass for about 300 yards. The scattered parties of Dervishes fell back and melted away, and only one straggling line of men in dark blue waited motionless a quarter of a mile to the left front. They were scarcely a hundred strong. The regiment formed into line of squadron columns, and continued at a walk until within 300 yards of this small body of Dervishes. The firing behind the ridges had stopped. There was complete silence, intensified by the recent tumult. Far beyond the thin blue row of Dervishes the fugitives were visible streaming into Omdurman. And should these few devoted men impede a regiment? Yet it were wiser to examine their position from the other flank before slipping a squadron at them. The heads of the squadrons wheeled slowly to the left, and the Lancers, breaking into a trot, began to cross the Dervish front in column of troops. Thereupon and with one accord the blue-clad men dropped on their knees, and there burst out a loud crackling fire of musketry. It was hardly possible to miss such a target at such a range. Horses and men fell at once. The only course was plain and welcome to all. The Colonel, nearer than his regiment, already saw what lay behind the skirmishers. He ordered 'Right wheel into line' to be sounded. The trumpet jerked out a shrill note, heard faintly above the trampling of the horses and the noise of the rifles. On the instant all the sixteen troops swung round and locked up into a long galloping line, and the 21st Lancers were committed to their first charge in war.

Two hundred and fifty yards away the dark-blue men were firing madly in a thin film of light-blue smoke. Their bullets struck the hard gravel into the air, and the troopers, to shield their faces from the stinging dust, bowed their helmets forward, like the Cuirassiers at Waterloo. The pace was fast and the distance short. Yet, before it was half covered, the whole aspect of the affair changed. A deep crease in the ground—a dry watercourse, a khor—appeared where all had seemed smooth, level plain; and from it there sprang, with the suddenness of a pantomime effect and a high-pitched yell, a dense white mass of men nearly as long as our front and about twelve deep. A score of horsemen and a dozen bright flags rose as if by magic from the earth. Eager warriors sprang forward to anticipate the shock. The rest stood firm to meet it. The Lancers acknowledged the apparition only by an increase of pace. Each man wanted sufficient momentum to drive through such a solid line. The flank troops, seeing that they overlapped, curved inwards like the horns of a moon. But the whole event was a matter of seconds. The riflemen, firing bravely to the last, were swept head over heels into the khor, and jumping down with them, at full gallop and in the closest order, the British squadrons struck the fierce brigade with one loud furious shout. The collision was prodigious. Nearly thirty lancers, men and horses, and at least two hundred Arabs were overthrown. The shock was stunning to both sides, and for perhaps ten wonderful seconds no man heeded his enemy. Terrified horses wedged in the crowd, bruised and shaken men, sprawling in heaps, struggled, dazed and stupid, to their feet, panted, and looked about them. Several fallen Lancers had even time to remount. Meanwhile the impetus of the cavalry carried them on. As a rider tears through a bullfinch, the officers forced their way through the press; and as an iron rake might be drawn through a heap of shingle, so the regiment followed. They shattered the Dervish array, and, their pace reduced to a walk, scrambled out of the khor on the further side, leaving a score of troopers behind them, and dragging on with the charge more than a thousand Arabs. Then, and not till then, the killing began; and thereafter each man saw the world along his lance, under his guard, or through the back-sight of his pistol; and each had his own strange tale to tell.

Stubborn and unshaken infantry hardly ever meet stubborn and unshaken cavalry. Either the infantry run away and are cut down in flight, or they keep their heads and destroy nearly all the horsemen by their musketry. On this occasion two living walls had actually crashed together. The Dervishes fought manfully. They tried to hamstring the horses. They fired their rifles, pressing the muzzles into the very bodies of their opponents. They cut reins and stirrup-leathers. They flung their throwing-spears with great dexterity. They tried every device of cool, determined men practised in war and familiar with cavalry; and, besides, they swung sharp, heavy swords which bit deep. The hand-to-hand fighting on the further side of the khor lasted for perhaps one minute. Then the horses got into their stride again, the pace increased, and the Lancers drew out from among their antagonists. Within two minutes of the collision every living man was clear of the Dervish mass. All who had fallen were cut at with swords till they stopped quivering, but no artistic mutilations were attempted.

Two hundred yards away the regiment halted, rallied, faced about, and in less than five minutes were re-formed and ready for a second charge. The men were anxious to cut their way back through their enemies. We were alone together—the cavalry regiment and the Dervish brigade. The ridge hung like a curtain between us and the army. The general battle was forgotten, as it was unseen. This was a private quarrel. The other might have been a massacre; but here the fight was fair, for we too fought with sword and spear. Indeed the advantage of ground and numbers lay with them. All prepared to settle the debate at once and for ever. But some realization of the cost of our wild ride began to come to those who were responsible. Riderless horses galloped across the plain. Men, clinging to their saddles, lurched helplessly about, covered with blood from perhaps a dozen wounds. Horses, streaming from tremendous gashes, limped and staggered with their riders. In 120 seconds five officers, 65 men, and 119 horses out of fewer than 400 had been killed or wounded.

The Dervish line, broken by the charge, began to re-form at once. They closed up, shook themselves together, and prepared with constancy and courage for another shock. But on military considerations it was desirable to turn them out of the khor first and thus deprive them of their vantage-ground. The regiment again drawn up, three squadrons in line and the fourth in column, now wheeled to the right, and, galloping round the Dervish flank, dismounted and opened a heavy fire with their magazine carbines. Under the pressure of this fire the enemy changed front to meet the new attack, so that both sides were formed at right angles to their original lines. When the Dervish change of front was completed, they began to advance against the dismounted men. But the fire was accurate, and there can be little doubt that the moral effect of the charge had been very great, and that these brave enemies were no longer unshaken. Be this as it may, the fact remains that they retreated swiftly, though in good order, towards the ridge of Surgham Hill, where the Khalifa's Black Flag still waved, and the 21st Lancers remained in possession of the ground—and of their dead.

The Dervishes were weak in cavalry, and had scarcely 2,000 horsemen on the field. About 400 of these, mostly the personal retainers of the various Emirs, were formed into an irregular regiment and attached to the flag of Ali-Wad-Helu. Now when these horsemen perceived that there was no more hope of victory, they arranged themselves in a solid mass and charged the left of MacDonald's brigade. The distance was about 500 yards, and, wild as was the firing of the Soudanese, it was evident that they could not possibly succeed. Nevertheless, many carrying no weapon in their hands, and all urging their horses to their utmost speed, they rode unflinchingly to certain death. All were killed and fell as they entered the zone of fire—three, twenty, fifty, two hundred, sixty, thirty, five and one out beyond them all—a brown smear across the sandy plain. A few riderless horses alone broke through the ranks of the infantry.

After the failure of the attack from Kerreri the whole Anglo-Egyptian army advanced westward, in a line of bayonets and artillery nearly two miles long, and drove the Dervishes before them into the desert, so that they could by no means rally or re-form. The Egyptian cavalry, who had returned along the river, formed line on the right of the infantry in readiness to pursue. At half past eleven Sir H. Kitchener shut up his glasses, and, remarking that he thought the enemy had been given 'a good dusting', gave the order for the brigades to resume their interrupted march on Omdurman—a movement which was possible, now that the forces in the plain were beaten. The brigadiers thereupon stopped the firing, massed their commands in convenient formations, and turned again towards the south and the city. The Lincolnshire Regiment remained detached as a rearguard.

Meanwhile the great Dervish army, who had advanced at sunrise in hope and courage, fled in utter rout, pursued by the Egyptian cavalry, harried by the 21st Lancers, and leaving more than 9,000 warriors dead and even greater numbers wounded behind them.

Thus ended the battle of Omdurman—the most signal triumph ever gained by the arms of science over barbarians. Within the space of five hours the strongest and best-armed savage army yet arrayed against a modern European Power had been destroyed and dispersed, with hardly any difficulty, comparatively small risk, and insignificant loss to the victors.

The River War

It is hard enough to understand the politics of one's own country; it is almost impossible to understand those of foreign countries.

There is no finer investment for any community than putting milk into babies.

In a long and varied life I have constantly watched and tried to measure the moods and inspirations of the British people. There is no foe they will not face. There is no hardship they cannot endure. Whether the test be sharp and short or long and wearisome, they can

52

take it. What they do not forgive is false promises and vain boastings.

We must beware of needless innovations, especially when guided by logic.

Martial law is no law at all. Martial law is brute force. Of course all martial law is illegal, and an attempt to introduce illegalities into martial law, which is not military law, is like attempting to add salt water to the sea.

The armoured train proceeded about fourteen miles towards the enemy and got as far as Chieveley station without a sign of opposition or indeed of life or movement on the broad undulations of the Natal landscape. We stopped for a few moments at Chieveley to report our arrival at this point by telegraph to the General. No sooner had we done this than we saw, on a hill between us and home which overlooked the line at about 600 yards distance, a number of small figures moving about and hurrying forward. Certainly they were Boers. Certainly they were behind us. What would they be doing with the railway line? There was not an instant to lose. We started immediately on our return journey. As we approached the hill, I was standing on a box with my head and shoulders above the steel plating of the rear armoured truck. I saw a cluster of Boers on the crest. Suddenly three wheeled things appeared among them, and instantly bright flashes of light opened and shut ten or twelve times. A huge white ball of smoke sprang into being and tore out into a cone, only as it seemed a few feet above my head. It was shrapnel—the first I had ever seen in war, and very nearly the last! The steel sides of the truck tanged with a patter of bullets. There was a crash from the front of the train, and a series of sharp explosions. The railway line curved round the base of the hill on a steep down gradient, and under the stimulus of the enemy's fire, as well as of the slope, our pace increased enormously. The Boer artillery (two guns and a pom-pom) had only time for one discharge before we were round the corner out of their sight. It had flashed across my mind that there must be some trap farther on. I was just turning to Haldane to suggest that someone should scramble along the train to make the engine-driver reduce speed, when suddenly there was a tremendous shock, and he and I and all the soldiers in the truck were pitched head over heels on to its floor. The armoured train travelling at not less than forty miles an hour had been thrown off the metals by some obstruction, or by some injury to the line.

In our truck no one was seriously hurt, and it took but a few seconds for me to scramble to my feet and look over the top of the armour. The train lay in a valley about 1,200 yards on the homeward side of the enemy's hill. On the top of this hill were scores of figures running forward and throwing themselves down in the grass, from which there came almost immediately an accurate and heavy rifle fire. The bullets whistled overhead and rang and splattered on the steel plates like a hailstorm. I got down from my perch, and Haldane and I debated what to do. It was agreed that he with the little naval gun and his Dublin Fusiliers in the rear truck should endeavour to keep down the enemy's firing, and that I should go and see what had happened to the train, what was the damage to the line, and whether there was any chance of repairing it or clearing the wreckage out of the way.

I nipped out of the truck accordingly and ran along

54

the line to the head of the train. The engine was still on the rails. The first truck, an ordinary bogy, had turned completely head over heels, killing and terribly injuring some of the platelayers who were upon it; but it lay quite clear of the track. The next two armoured trucks, which contained the Durban Light Infantry, were both derailed, one still upright and the other on its side. They lay jammed against each other in disorder, blocking the homeward path of the rest. Behind the overturned trucks the Durban Light Infantry men, bruised, shaken, and some severely injured, had found a temporary shelter. The enemy's fire was continuous, and soon there mingled with the rifles the bang of the field-guns and the near explosion of their shells. We were in the toils of the enemy.

As I passed the engine another shrapnel burst immediately as it seemed overhead, hurling its contents with a rasping rush through the air. The driver at once sprang out of the cab and ran to the shelter of the overturned trucks. His face cut open by a splinter streamed with blood, and he complained in bitter, futile indignation. 'He was a civilian. What did they think he was paid for? To be killed by a bombshell—not he? He would not stay another minute.' It looked as if his excitement and misery—he was dazed by the blow on his head—would prevent him from working the engine further, and as only he understood the machinery, the hope of escape would thus be cut off. So I told him that no man was hit twice on the same day: that a wounded man who continued to do his duty was always rewarded for distinguished gallantry, and that he might never have this chance again. On this he pulled himself together, wiped the blood off his face, climbed back into the cab of his engine, and thereafter obeyed every order which I gave him.

I was very lucky in the hour that followed not to be hit. It was necessary for me to be almost continuously moving up and down the train or standing in the open, telling the engine-driver what to do.

But while these events had been taking place everything else had been in movement. I had not retraced my steps 200 yards when, instead of Haldane and his company, two figures in plain clothes appeared upon the line. 'Platelayers!' I said to myself, and then with a surge of realization, 'Boers!' My mind retains its impressions of these tall figures, full of energy, clad in dark, flapping clothes, with slouch, storm-driven hats, poising on their levelled rifles hardly a hundred yards away. I turned again and ran back towards the engine, the two Boers firing as I ran between the metals. Their bullets, sucking to right and left, seemed to miss only by inches. We were in a small cutting with banks about six feet high on either side. I flung myself against the bank of the cutting. It gave no cover. Another glance at the two figures; one was now kneeling to aim. Movement seemed the only chance. Again I darted forward: again two soft kisses sucked in the air; but nothing struck me. This could not endure. I must get out of the cutting—that damnable corridor! I jigged to the left, and scrambled up the bank. The earth sprang up beside me. I got through the wire fence unhurt. Outside the cutting was a tiny depression. I crouched in this, struggling to get my breath again.

Fifty yards away was a small platelayer's cabin of masonry; there was cover there. About 200 yards away was the rocky gorge of the Blue Krantz River; there was plenty of cover there. I determined to make a dash for the river. I rose to my feet. Suddenly on the other side of the railway, separated from me by the rails and two uncut wire fences, I saw a horseman galloping furiously, a tall, dark figure, holding his rifle in his right hand. He pulled up his horse almost in its own length and shaking the rifle at me shouted a loud command. We were forty yards apart. That morning I had taken with me, Correspondent-status notwithstanding, my Mauser pistol. I thought I could kill this man, and after the treatment I had received I earnestly desired to do so. I put my hand to my belt, the pistol was not there. When engaged in clearing the line, getting in and out of the engine, etc., I had taken it off. It came safely home on the engine. I have it now! But at this moment I was quite unarmed. Meanwhile, I suppose in about the time this takes to tell, the Boer horseman, still seated on his horse, had covered me with his rifle. The animal stood stock still, so did he, and so did I. I looked towards the river, I looked towards the platelayer's hut. The Boer continued to look along his sights. I thought there were absolutely no chance of escape, if he fired he would surely hit me, so I held up my hands and surrendered myself a prisoner of war.

'When one is alone and unarmed,' said the great Napoleon, in words which flowed into my mind in the poignant minutes that followed, 'a surrender may be pardoned.' Still he might have missed; and the Blue Krantz ravine was very near and the two wire fences were still uncut. However, the deed was done. Thereupon my captor lowered his rifle and beckoned to me to come across to him. I obeyed. I walked through the wire fences and across the line and stood by his side. He sprang off his horse and began firing in the direction of the bridge upon the retreating engine and a few straggling British figures. Then when the last had disappeared he re-mounted and at his side I tramped back towards the spot where I had left Captain Haldane and his company. I saw none of them. They were already prisoners. I noticed that it was raining hard. As I plodded through the high grass by the side of my captor a disquieting and timely reflection came into my mind. I had two clips of Mauser ammunition, each holding ten rounds, in two little breast pockets one on each side of my khaki coat. These cartridges were the same as I had used at Omdurman, and were the only kind supplied for the Mauser pistol. They were what are called 'soft-nosed bullets'. I had never given them a thought until now; and it was borne in upon me that they might be a very dangerous possession. I dropped the right-hand clip on the ground without being seen. I had got the left-hand clip in my hand and was about to drop it, when my captor looked down sharply and said in English, 'What have you got there?'

'What is it?' I said, opening the palm of my hand, 'I picked it up.'

He took it, looked at it and threw it away. We continued to plod on until we reached the general gang of prisoners and found ourselves speedily in the midst of many hundreds of mounted Boers who streamed into view, in long columns of twos and threes, many holding umbrellas over their heads in the pouring rain.

Such is the episode of the armoured train and the story of my capture on November 15, 1899.

My Early Life

In the Middle East you have arid countries. In East Africa you have dripping countries. There is the greatest difficulty to get anything to grow on the one place, and the greatest difficulty to prevent things smothering and choking you by their hurried growth in the other. In the African Colonies you have a docile, tractable population, who only require to be well and wisely treated to develop great economic capacity and utility; whereas

58

the regions of the Middle East are unduly stocked with peppery, pugnacious, proud politicians and theologians, who happen to be at the same time extremely well armed and extremely hard up.

It is vain to imagine that the mere perception or declaration of right principles, whether in one country or in many countries, will be of any value unless they are supported by those qualities of civic virtue and manly courage—aye, and by those instruments and agencies of force and science which in the last resort must be the defence of right and reason.

In dealing with nationalities, nothing is more fatal than a dodge. Wrongs will be forgiven, sufferings and losses will be forgiven or forgotten, battles will be remembered only as they recall the martial virtues of the combatants; but anything like chicane, anything like a trick, will always rankle.

'Tell the truth to the British people.' They are a tough people, a robust people. They may be a bit offended at the moment, but if you have told them exactly what is going on, you have insured yourself against complaints and reproaches which are very unpleasant when they come home on the morrow of some disillusion.

I have no objection to a proper use of strong language, but a certain amount of art and a certain amount of selective power is needed, if the effect is to be produced.

It is a very fine thing to refuse an invitation, but it is a good thing to wait till you get it first.

Someone says it's a lie. Well, I am reminded by that of the remark of the witty Irishman who said: 'There are a terrible lot of lies going about the world, and the worst of it is that half of them are true.'

You don't want to knock a man down except to pick him up in a better frame of mind.

'Together with Captain Haldane and Lieutenant Brockie I made an abortive attempt at escape, not pushed with any decision, on December 11. There was no difficulty in getting into the circular office. But to climb out of it over the wall was a hazard of the sharpest character. Anyone doing so must at the moment he was on the top of the wall be plainly visible to the sentries fifteen yards away, if they were in the right place and happened to look! Whether the sentries would challenge or fire depended entirely upon their individual dispositions, and no one could tell what they would do. Nevertheless, I was determined that nothing should stop my taking the plunge the next day. As the 12th wore away my fears crystallized more and more into desperation. In the evening, after my two friends had made an attempt, but had not found the moment propitious, I strolled across the quadrangle and secreted myself in the circular office. Through an aperture in the metal casing of which it was built I watched the sentries. For some time they remained stolid and obstructive. Then all of a sudden one turned and walked up to his comrade, and they began to talk. Their backs were turned.

'Now or never! I stood on a ledge, seized the top of the wall with my hands, and drew myself up. Twice I let myself down again in sickly hesitation, and then with a third resolve scrambled up and over. My waistcoat got entangled with the ornamental metal-work on the top. I had to pause for an appreciable moment to extricate myself. In this posture I had one parting glimpse of the sentries still talking with their backs turned fifteen yards away. One of them was lighting his cigarette, and I remember the glow on the inside of his hands as a distinct impression which my mind recorded. Then I lowered myself lightly down into the adjoining garden and crouched among the shrubs. I was free! The first step had been taken, and it was irrevocable. It now remained to await the arrival of my comrades. The bushes in the garden gave a good deal of cover, and in the moonlight their shadows fell dark on the ground. I lay here for an hour in great impatience and anxiety. People were continually moving about in the garden, and once a man came and apparently looked straight at me only a few yards away. Where were the others? Why did they not make the attempt?

'Suddenly I heard a voice from within the quadrangle say, quite loud, "All up." I crawled back to the wall. Two officers were walking up and down inside, jabbering Latin words, laughing and talking all manner of nonsense—amid which I caught my name. I risked a cough. One of the officers immediately began to chatter alone. The other said, slowly and clearly, "They cannot get out. The sentry suspects. It's all up. Can you get back again?" But now all my fears fell from me at once. To go back was impossible. I could not hope to climb the wall unnoticed. There was no helpful ledge on the outside. Fate pointed onwards. Besides, I said to myself, "Of course, I shall be recaptured, but I will at least have a run for my money." I said to the officers, "I shall go on alone."

'Now I was in the right mood for these undertakings —failure being almost certain, no odds against success affected me. All risks were less than the certainty. A glance at the plan will show that the gate which led into the road was only a few yards from another sentry. I said to myself, "Toujours de l'audace," put my hat on my head, strode into the middle of the garden, walked past the windows of the house without any attempt at concealment, and went through the gate and turned to the left. I passed the sentry at less than five yards. Most of them knew me by sight. Whether he looked at me or not I do not know, for I never turned my head. I restrained with the utmost difficulty an impulse to run. But after walking a hundred yards and hearing no challenge, I knew that the second obstacle had been surmounted. I was at large in Pretoria.

'I walked on leisurely through the night, humming a tune and choosing the middle of the road. The streets were full of burghers, but they paid no attention to me. Gradually I reached the suburbs, and on a little bridge I sat down to reflect and consider. I was in the heart of the enemy's country. I knew no one to whom I could apply for succour. Nearly three hundred miles stretched between me and Delagoa Bay. My escape must be known at dawn. Pursuit would be immediate. Yet all exits were barred. The town was picketed, the country was patrolled, the trains were searched, the line was guarded. I wore a civilian brown flannel suit. I had seventy-five pounds in my pocket and four slabs of chocolate, but the compass and the map which might have guided me, the opium tablets and meat lozenges which should have sustained me, were in my friends' pockets in the State Model Schools. Worst of all, I could not speak a word of Dutch or Kaffir, and how was I to get food or direction?

'But when hope had departed, fear had gone as well. I formed a plan. I would find the Delagoa Bay Railway. Without map or compass, I must follow that in spite of the pickets. I looked at the stars. Orion shone brightly. Scarcely a year before he had guided me when lost in the desert to the banks of the Nile. He had given me water. Now he should lead to freedom. I could not endure the want of either.

'After walking south for half a mile I struck the railway. Was it the line to Delagoa Bay or the Pietersburg branch? If it were the former, it should run east. But, so far as I could see, this line ran northwards. Still, it might only be winding its way out among the hills. I resolved to follow it. The night was delicious. A cool breeze fanned my face, and a wild feeling of exhilaration took hold of me. At any rate, I was free, if only for an hour. That was something. The fascination of the adventure grew. Unless the stars in their courses fought for me, I could not escape. Where, then, was the need for caution, I marched briskly along the line. Here and there the lights of a picket fire gleamed. Every bridge had its watchers. But I passed them all, making very short detours at the dangerous places, and really taking scarcely any precautions. Perhaps that was the reason I succeeded.

My Early Life

Providence has ordained that human beings should have short memories, and pain and anxiety are soon forgotten. But are we always to oscillate between panic and torpor?

In war, if you are not able to beat your enemy at his own game, it is nearly always better to adopt some striking variant, and not to be content merely with doing the same thing as your enemy is doing, only not doing it quite so well or on quite so large a scale.

63

I now plunged into a by-election [Oldham, 1900. Ed.] attended by the fullest publicity attaching to such episodes. I have fought up to the present fourteen contested elections, which take about a month of one's life apiece. It is melancholy, when one reflects upon our brief span, to think that no less than fourteen months of life have been passed in this wearing clatter. By-elections, of which I have had five, are even worse than ordinary elections because of all the cranks and faddists of the country and all their associates and all the sponging 'uplift' organizations fasten upon the wretched candidate. If he is a supporter of the administration, all the woes of the world, all the shortcomings of human society in addition, are laid upon him, and he is vociferously urged to say what he is going to do about them.

My Early Life

I have noticed that whenever a distinguished politician declares that a particular question is above Party, what he really means is that everybody, without distinction of Party, shall vote for him.

The dignity of a Prime Minister, like a lady's virtue, was not susceptible of partial diminution.

A distinction should be drawn at the outset between two kinds of political inconsistency. First, a statesman in contact with the moving current of events and anxious to keep the ship on an even keel and steer a steady course may lean all his weight now on one side and now on the other. His arguments in each case when contrasted can be shown to be not only very different in character, but contradictory in spirit and opposite in direction; yet his object will throughout have remained the same. His resolve, his wishes, his outlook may have been unchanged; his methods may be verbally irreconcilable. We cannot call this inconsistency. The only way a man can remain consistent amid changing circumstances is to change with them while preserving the same dominating purpose.

A statesman should always try to do what he believes is best in the long view for his country, and he should not be dissuaded from so acting by having to divorce himself from a great body of doctrine to which he formerly sincerely adhered.

Thoughts and Adventures

I am reminded of the professor who, in his declining hours, was asked by his devoted pupils for his final counsel. He replied, 'Verify your quotations.'

Mr. Bernard Shaw was one of my earliest antipathies. Indeed, almost my first literary effusion, written when I was serving as a subaltern in India in 1897 (it never saw the light of day), was a ferocious onslaught upon him, and upon an article which he had written disparaging and deriding the British Army in some minor way. Four or five years passed before I made his acquaintance. My mother always in agreeable contact with artistic and dramatic circles, took me to luncheon with him. I was instantly attracted by the sparkle and gaiety of his conversation, and impressed by his eating only fruit and vegetables, and drinking only water. I rallied him on the latter habit, asking : 'Do you really never drink any wine at all?' 'I am hard enough to keep in order as it is,' he replied. Perhaps he had heard of my youthful prejudice against him.

In later years, and especially after the war, I can recall several pleasant and, to me, memorable talks

65

on politics, particularly about Ireland and about Socialism. I think these encounters cannot have been displeasing to him, for he was kind enough to give me a copy of his Magnum Opus, *The Intelligent Woman's Guide to Socialism,* remarking (subsequently and erroneously), 'It is a sure way to prevent you reading it.' At any rate, I possess a lively image of this bright, nimble, fierce, and comprehending being, Jack Frost dancing bespangled in the sunshine, which I should be very sorry to lose.

Great Contemporaries

If the truth must be told, our British island has not had much help in its troubles from Mr. Bernard Shaw. When nations are fighting for life, when the palace in which the jester dwells not uncomfortably is itself assailed, and everyone from prince to groom is fighting on the battlements, the jester's jokes echo only through deserted halls, and his witticisms and condemnations, distributed evenly between friend and foe, jar the ear of hurrying messengers, of mourning women and wounded men. The titter ill accords with the tocsin, or the motley with the bandages.

Great Contemporaries

I look forward to the universal establishment of minimum standards of life and labour, and their progressive elevation as the increasing energies of production may permit. I do not think that Liberalism in any circumstances can cut itself off from this fertile field of social effort, and I would recommend you not to be scared in discussing any of these proposals, just because some old woman comes along and tells you they are Socialistic.

Speech at Glasgow, October 11, 1906

The casual unskilled labourer who is habitually under-employed, who is lucky to get three, or at the outside four days' work in the week, who may often be out of a job for three or four weeks at a time, who in bad times goes under altogether, and who in good times has no hope of security and no incentive to thrift, whose whole life and the lives of his wife and children are embarked in a sort of blind, desperate, fatalistic gamble with circumstances beyond his comprehension or control, that this poor man, this terrible and pathetic figure, is not as a class the result of accident or chance, is not casual because he wishes to be casual, is not casual as the consequence of some temporary disturbance soon put right. No; the casual labourer is here because he is wanted here. He is here in answer to a perfectly well-defined demand. He is here as the result of economic causes which have been too long unregulated. He is not the natural product, he is an article manufactured, called into being, to suit the requirements, in the Prime Minister's telling phrases, of all industries at particular times and of particular industries at all times.

Kinnaird Hall, Dundee, October 10, 1908

On the morning of December 17, 1910, all England was startled and astonished by the accounts which filled the newspapers of an extraordinary crime. At half-past ten on the previous night a Mr. Isenstein, the owner of a fancy-goods shop in Houndsditch, became alarmed by mysterious rappings at the back of his premises. These rappings had been noticed a fortnight earlier, and the police had already made inquiries about them. But now they were louder and nearer, and evidently came from the house next door. Mr. Isenstein sent for the police. A party of six officers and constables arrived; two were posted at the rear of the premises, and the sergeant, followed by three others, went up to the door of the house whence the rapping was believed to proceed and knocked. Following the custom which, till then, had long been almost invariable in England, all the police were unarmed. The door was opened about six inches by a man.

'Have you been working here?' asked the sergeant.

No answer.

'Do you understand English? Have you anyone in the house who can speak English?'

The man closed the door all but an inch, and leaving the question unanswered, disappeared upstairs. The sergeant pushed the door open and entered a gas-lighted room. There seemed no special reason for precautions. The sergeant was only making an ordinary police inquiry, and he stood for a minute waiting. It was his last. Suddenly a door was flung open, a pistol-shot rang out, and the sergeant fell in the doorway. Another shot, this time from the dark stairway, drove the advancing police from the door; through that door a man's hand with a long automatic pistol appeared, a succession of shots was fired, and in a few seconds all four constables lay dead, dying or wounded in the street. A figure sprang from the house, firing right and left. There remained only Constable Choate, unarmed and already wounded. This officer unhesitatingly grappled with the assassin, and, in spite of being twice more shot in the body, was still holding him when he was shot again from behind by another of the criminals and fell dying from twelve separate wounds. The gang of murderers shook off the pursuit of the sixth policeman at the rear of the premises and disappeared into the darkness and movement of London by night, leaving for the moment neither trace nor clue.

The subsequent police investigation showed that a

systematic burglary was being planned, not against Mr. Isenstein's premises, but against those of an adjoining jeweller, where £30,000 worth of goods was kept locked up in a safe. The brick wall between the buildings had been nearly tunnelled through, and in the tunnel were found complete and perfect burglars' outfits for forcing a safe with an acetylene flame.

At three o'clock the next morning a doctor was summoned by two women to attend a young man who gave the name of George Gardstein, and explained that he had been shot in the back by mistake with a revolver by a friend three hours before. This man, whose name was Morountzef, was the criminal who killed the police sergeant, and it appeared that in the scuffle with Constable Choate he had been pierced through the lungs and stomach by one of the bullets which had traversed the body of the heroic officer. He expired before morning, leaving behind him a Browning automatic pistol, a dagger, and a violin.

Such in brief outline was the story which the newspapers of the next few days gradually unfolded. We were clearly in the presence of a class of crime and a type of criminal which for generations had found no counterpart in England. The ruthless ferocity of the criminals, their intelligence, their unerring marksmanship, their modern weapons and equipment, all disclosed the characteristics of the Russian Anarchist. It was ascertained in the days that followed that the murderers belonged to a small colony of about twenty Letts from Baltic Russia, who, under the leadership of an Anarchist known as 'Peter the Painter', had ensconced themselves in the heart of London. It was in fact, in the language of later years, a 'germ cell' of murder, anarchy, and revolution. These fierce beings, living, as it was said, 'just like animals,' were pursuing their predatory schemes and dark conspiracies. Although they were thieves and murderers for personal ends, all their actions had also a political character. 'Peter the Painter' was one of those wild beasts, who, in later years, amid the convulsions of the Great War, were to devour and ravage the Russian State and people.

Wrath and indignation at this monstrous crime were general throughout the country. The whole resources of Scotland Yard were concentrated on the pursuit of the criminals. As Home Secretary I immediately ordered the police to be provided with the best pattern of automatic pistol then procurable. The brave constables who had fallen in the discharge of their duty were accorded a public funeral, and their coffins, covered with the Union Jack, lay in St. Paul's Cathedral during a solemn memorial service attended by the dignitaries of the City of London.

There followed an interlude while all the resources of which a civilized community can dispose were directed to hunting down the criminals.

At about ten o'clock on the morning of January 3 I was in my bath, when I was surprised by an urgent knocking at the door.

'There is a message from the Home Office on the telephone absolutely immediate.'

Dripping wet and shrouded in a towel I hurried to the instrument, and received the following news:

'The Anarchists who murdered the police have been surrounded in a house in the East End—No. 100 Sidney Street—and are firing on the police with automatic pistols. They have shot one man and appear to have plenty of ammunition. Authority is requested to send for troops to arrest or kill them.'

I replied at once, giving the necessary permission and directing the police to use whatever force was necessary.

In about twenty minutes I was at the Home Office. There I found my principal adviser, Mr. Ernley Blackwell, who told me that no further information had been received, except that the Anarchists had been effectually surrounded, but were still firing in all directions. No one knew how many Anarchists there were or what measures were going to be taken. In these circumstances I thought it my duty to see what was going on myself, and my advisers concurred in the propriety of such a step. I must, however, admit that convictions of duty were supported by a strong sense of curiosity which perhaps it would have been well to keep in check.

We started at once in a motor-car. Down the Strand, through the City towards Houndsditch, until at length at about noon we reached the point where all traffic was stopped. We got out of the car. There was a considerable crowd of angry and alarmed people, and I noticed the unusual spectacle of Metropolitan constables armed with shotguns hastily procured from a local gunsmith. The attitude of the crowd was not particularly friendly, and there were several cries of 'Oo let 'em in?' in allusion to the refusal of the Liberal Government to introduce drastic laws restricting the immigration of aliens. Just at this moment, however, a shot rang out perhaps a couple of hundred yards away, followed by another and another, until there was a regular fusillade. Accompanied by an inspector, we proceeded down the empty street, turned a corner, turned another corner, and reached a group of policemen, several of whom were armed, and a number of onlookers and journalists who had found themselves within the police cordon when it was originally closed and had been permitted to remain. Another street ran at right angles across our path. Up this street fifty or sixty yards to the left was the house (No. 100) in which the murderers had barricaded themselves. On the opposite side in front of us, police, Scots Guardsmen, and spectators were crouching behind the projecting corners of the buildings; and from both sides of the street, from the street itself, and from numerous windows, policemen and other persons were firing rifles, pistols, and shotguns with increasing frequency at the house which harboured the desperadoes. These replied every minute or two, shooting sometimes up and down the street and sometimes at their assailants in front. The bullets struck the brickwork and ricocheted hither and thither. We have since become only too familiar with scenes of this kind, and the spectacle of street fighting has long lost its novelty in Europe. But nothing of the sort had ever been seen within living memory in quiet, law-abiding, comfortable England; and from this point of view at least my journey was well repaid.

But the situation almost immediately became embarrassing. Some of the police officers were anxious to storm the building at once with their pistols. Others rightly thought it better to take more time and to avoid the almost certain loss of three or four valuable lives. It was no part of my duty to take personal control or to give executive decisions. From my chair in the Home Office I could have sent any order and it would have been immediately acted on, but it was not for me to interfere with those who were in charge on the spot. Yet, on the other hand, my position of authority, far above them all, attracted inevitably to itself direct responsibility. I saw now that I should have done much better to have remained quietly in my office. On the other hand, it was impossible to get into one's car and drive away while matters stood in such great uncertainty, and moreover, were extremely interesting.

Being anxious to have a direct view of the besieged house, I now crossed the street and took shelter in the doorway of a warehouse on the opposite side. Here I found Lord Knutsford, the Chairman of the London Hospital, and together we watched the closing scenes of the drama.

Plans were now made to storm the building from several sides at once. One party, emerging from the next-door house, was to rush the front door and charge up the stairs; another party of police and soldiers would break into the second floor at the back through a window; a third, smashing-in the roof, would leap down on the assassins from above. There could be no doubt about the result of such an attack, but it certainly seemed that loss of life would be caused, not only by the fire of the Anarchists, but also from shots fired by the attackers in the confusion. My own instincts turned at once to a direct advance up the staircase behind a steel plate or shield, and search was made in the foundries of the neighbourhood for one of a suitable size. Meanwhile, however, the problem settled itself. At about half past one a wisp of smoke curled out of the shattered upper windows of the besieged house, and in a few minutes it was plainly on fire. The conflagration gained apace, burning downwards. To the crackling of wood succeeded the roar of flames. Still the Anarchists, descending storey by storey, kept up their fire, and bullets continued to strike the brickwork of the surrounding houses and pavement.

Now occurred a curious incident, which, for the first time, made my presence on the spot useful. The ordinary functions of British life had been proceeding inflexibly to within a few feet of the danger-zone, and the postman on his rounds actually delivered his letters at the house next door. Suddenly, with a stir and a clatter, up came the fire brigade, scattering the crowds gathered on the approaches to the scene and thrusting through them until they reached the police cordon at the beginning of the danger-zone. The inspector of police forbade further progress, and the fire brigade officer declared it his duty to advance. A fire was raging, and he was bound to extinguish it. Anarchists, automatic pistols, danger-zones, nothing of this sort was mentioned in the Regulations of the London Fire Brigade. When the police officer pointed out that his men would be shot down, he replied simply that orders were orders and that he had no alternative. I now intervened to settle the dispute, at one moment quite heated. I told the fire-brigade officer on my authority as Home Secretary, that the house was to be allowed to burn down and that he was to stand by in readiness to prevent the conflagration from spreading. I then returned to my coign of vantage on the opposite side of the road.

The flames were now beginning to invade the ground floor of the doomed house. Some minutes had passed without a shot being fired by the Anarchists. No human being could live longer in the building. Everyone expected to see the Anarchists—how many there were was not known for certain—sally out, pistol in hand, into the open street. A hundred rifles, revolvers, and shotguns were levelled at the smouldering doorway. The minutes passed in intense excitement, and the flames invaded the whole ground floor. At last it became certain that these human fiends had perished. Suddenly, upon a spontaneous impulse which led everyone into the open, a detective inspector walked quickly to the door and kicked it open. I followed a few yards behind, accompanied by a police sergeant with a double-barrelled shotgun. There was nothing but smoke and flame inside the building. The firemen rushed forward into the empty street with their hoses, and behind them surged a crowd of soldiers, journalists, photographers, and spectators. It was already three o'clock, and leaving the now-dying fire to be dealt with by the fire brigade and the ruins to be searched by the police, I went home.

Besides the police inspector shot in the morning, a colour sergeant of the Guards and three civilians had been wounded by bullets, and a police sergeant struck, but not seriously injured, by a ricochet. Up to this moment no lives had been lost except those of the murderers. Alas, the day was not yet done! A falling wall injured five of the firemen, two in the most grave manner. There were found in the ruins of Sidney Street two charred bodies, one shot by a British bullet and one apparently suffocated by smoke. These were established to be the corpses of Fritz Svaars and Jacob Vogel, both members of 'Peter the Painter's' Anarchist gang, and both certainly concerned in the police murders. One Browning and two Mauser pistols and six gun-metal bomb-cases were found amid the ruins, together with many cartridges.

Thus ended the battle of Sidney Street. Of 'Peter the Painter' not a trace was ever found. He vanished completely. Rumour has repeatedly claimed him as one of the Bolshevik liberators and saviours of Russia. Certainly his qualities and record would well have fitted him to take an honoured place in that noble band. But of this rumour is alone the foundation.

Party controversy was then at its height in England, and I was much criticized in the newspapers and in Parliament for my share in this curious episode. Mr. Balfour in the House of Commons was especially sarcastic.

'We are concerned to observe,' he said in solemn tones, 'photographs in the illustrated newspapers of the Home Secretary in the danger-zone. I understand what the photographer was doing, but why the Home Secretary?'

And with this not altogether unjust reflection I may bring the story to an end.

Thoughts and Adventures

Time is a tremendous lever and a tremendous weapon either in peace or in war. In fact, I think in the government of states a judicious use of time is very often one of the most potent and effective weapons.

Commons, April 12, 1910

Averages, Magic of. There is exhilaration in the study of insurance questions because there is a sense of elaborating new and increased powers which have been devoted to the service of mankind. It is not only a question of order in the face of confusion. It is not only a question of collective strength of the nation to render effective the thrift and the exertions of the individual, but we bring in the magic of averages to the aid of the million.

Commons, May 25, 1911

Vulnerability. Alone among the great modern states, we can neither defend the soil upon which we live nor subsist upon its produce.

Commons, March 17, 1913

There are a few points on which I am not convinced. Of these, the greatest is the question of the use of submarines to sink merchant vessels. I do not believe this would ever be done by a civilized Power.

Memo to Lord Fisher, January 1, 1914

The nose of the bulldog has been slanted backwards so that he can breathe without letting go.

Description of naval strategy in 1914

In the year 1906 when I was Under-Secretary of State for the Colonies I received an invitation from the German Emperor to attend as his guest the Annual Manoeuvres of the German Army in Silesia. Having obtained the permission of the British Government, I set out for Breslau at the beginning of September, and was accommodated with other Imperial and official guests in the comfortable old-word 'Golden Goose' Hotel. The manoeuvres were on a great scale, a whole Army Corps and one completely-mobilized division at war strength being employed. Everything was managed with the usual German efficiency, and with rigid care in matters of the smallest detail. The large number of visitors, including of course representatives of all the armies in Europe, were handled and moved with the most minute consideration of rank and etiquette, and as far as the Emperor's own guests were concerned, an element of personal hospitality was mingled with the official ceremonial and routine. The week, while brilliant and deeply interesting, was most strenuous, and except sometimes on active service, I have hardly ever been so short of sleep. Every night there was a glittering full-dress banquet, at which the Emperor—or in his absence on the manoeuvre ground the Empress—presided. We went to bed shortly before midnight only to be aroused at 3 or 4 o'clock in the morning to join the special train which conveyed us to the particular point of the battle-field where the situation of the opposing armies could be studied. Here, as the first light paled the Eastern sky, we mounted our horses and, each accompanied by an officer of the German General Staff, set off wherever we liked to go. After 10 or 12 hours of riding about and watching the operations, we gathered again in the special train at some new point and got back to Breslau in time to dress for the next banquet, followed by an Imperial tattoo, another brief interlude of sleep, and another 4-o'clock-in-the-morning departure. Such was the cycle of our hours.

Magnificent was the spectacle of German military and Imperial splendour so brilliantly displayed to foreign eyes. Several scenes linger in my memory which illustrated the pomp and power of the German Empire. When the Emperor, resplendent in the uniform of the White Silesian Cuirassiers, rode through the streets of Breslau at the head of a sparkling cavalcade, he was rapturously welcomed by his dutiful subjects. A large portion of the road was lined, not by troops, but by many thousands of elderly men obviously belonging to the poorer classes, all dressed punctiliously in ancient black frock-coats and tall hats. These were the old soldiers, to whom special positions of honour were accorded, and indeed they formed a striking background of sombre civic strength to the white uniforms of the Emperor and his Cuirassiers.

In the Review which preceded the manoeuvres 50,000 horse, foot and artillery marched past the Emperor and his galaxy of kings and princes. The Infantry, regiment by regiment, in line of battalion quarter columns, reminded one more of great Atlantic rollers than human formations. Clouds of cavalry, avalanches of field guns and—at that time a novelty— squadrons of motor-cars (private and military) completed the array. For five hours the immense defilade continued. Yet this was only a twentieth of the armed strength of the regular German Army before mobilization; and the same martial display could have been produced simultaneously in every province of the Empire. I thought of our tiny British Army, in which the parade of a single division and a brigade of Cavalry at Aldershot was a notable event. I watched from time to time the thoughtful, sombre visage of the French Military Attaché, who sat on his horse beside me absorbed in reflections which it would not have been difficult to plumb. The very atmosphere was pervaded by a sense of inexhaustible and exuberant manhood and deadly panoply. The glories of this world and force abounding could not present a more formidable, and even stupefying, manifestation.

On the evening of this Review the Emperor gave his dinner to the Province. Three or four hundred Silesian functionaries and notables, together with the foreign guests, in uniforms of every colour and loaded with gold lace and decorations, assembled in a spacious hall.

The Emperor spoke with his usual facility and with the majesty that none could deny. The German staff officer at my side translated in a whisper sentence by sentence into excellent English. It was the year 1906, the Centenary of the Battle of Jena. 'A hundred years ago,' said William II, 'Germany was reduced to the abyss of ruin. Our armies were everywhere captured or dispersed, our fortresses taken, our Capital captured by hostile troops, the very structure of our State broken into fragments, long years of foreign domination ahead.' Only a hundred years ago! It seemed incredible that a single century, four fleeting generations, should have sufficed to raise the mighty fabric of power and wealth, energy and organization, of which we were the awe-struck witnesses. What an amazing contrast: 1806–1906! What a contrast also between the bounding fortunes of martial Germany and the slow-growing continuity of British national life, which after 900 years of immunity from foreign invasion still wore a modest and self-questioning garb. But more amazing still would have been the contrast if the curtains of the future could for a moment have been swept aside, and if that glittering throng could have perceived that scarcely ten years separated triumphant Germany from a collapse, subjugation and prostration, far more complete and lasting than any that had darkened the morrow of Jena.

The manoeuvres however, for all their impressive scale of mechanism revealed many questionable features to an instructed eye. Like others in the handful of British officers, who in various capacities were watching the operations, I had carried away from the South African veldt a very lively and modern sense of what rifle bullets could do. On the effects of the fire of large numbers of guns, we could only use our imagination. But where the power of the magazine rifle was concerned we felt sure we possessed a practical experience denied to the leaders of these trampling hosts. We watched with astonishment the movements of dense columns of men over bare slopes, within a few hundred yards of woods along whose entrenched outskirts lines of riflemen burned blank cartridges in unceasing fusillade. As the climax of the manoeuvres approached the opposing infantry masses came very close to one another. Presently we found them lying on the ground fifty yards apart in dense formation, bayonets fixed and the front ranks firing furiously. More astonishing still— on the order to charge being given, these placid phalanxes rose from the ground and still with bayonets fixed advanced through each other with perfect drill, and lay down dutifully on the other side toes to toes. Whatever else this might amount to, it did not form contact with reality at any point. Besides South Africa I had also vividly in my mind the Battle of Omdurman, where we had shot down quite easily, with hardly any loss, more than 11,000 Dervishes in formations much less dense, and at ranges far greater than those which were now on every side exhibited to our gaze. We had said to ourselves after Omdurman, 'This is the end of these sort of spectacles. There will never be such fools in the world again.'

Some inkling of the truth about modern fire had already began to circulate in the German Army. As we advanced over the rolling down, accompanying an attack delivered by a line of massed columns of infantry under the fire of at least 100 guns, and of thousands of happily harmless rifles, I noticed signs of unconcealed impatience among the German officers with whom I rode. A Princess, who in full uniform was leading her regiment, was in the easy assurance of Royal privilege indignantly 'outspoken'. 'What folly!' she exclaimed. 'It is madness. The Generals should all be dismissed.' And so on. But in the main everything passed off happily.

At the Grand Finale the Emperor led in person a charge of 30 or 40 squadrons of cavalry upon a long line of field guns in the centre of the enemy's position. We all galloped along in the greatest glee, and the surging waves of horsemen soon overwhelmed and swept through the rows of venomous-looking little cannons which presumed to confront them. 'Do you think it is all right?' we asked an Artillery officer whose battery the Umpire had loyally adjudged to be captured. 'Certainly it is all right,' he replied. 'They are His Majesty's own guns. Why shouldn't he capture them? It is an honour for us to serve His Majesty in this manner.' But there was a twinkle in his eye.

After the bugles had sounded the 'Cease Fire' over the wide plain, the great German Staff drew together round their War Lord on the summit of a little hill behind which a crowd of green-clad soldiers speedily erected a small wooden chalet for his Military Quarters in the field. The Emperor welcomed his personal guests with that unaffected and easy grace which was habitual to him, and added so much to his charm and popularity. He talked to foreign visitors with the freedom and manner of an agreeable host at an English country-house party, while all around the stiff uniformed figures of his Generals and Aides-de-Camp stood immobile and passive, each rooted to his particular spot. 'What do you think of this beautiful Silesia?' he asked me in his facile English. 'Fine country, isn't it? Well worth fighting for, and,' he added, 'well fought over. These fields are ankle-deep in blood. There,' pointing to the town of Liegnitz, 'is where Frederick fought his battle. Down there,' he indicated a wooded valley, 'is the Katsbach stream, where we beat the French in 1813 in our war of Liberation.' I made such comments as occurred to me. 'Have you seen everything you want? I wish you to see everything perfectly freely. Tell me, is there anything you have not seen that you would like to see? Have you seen my new gun?' I said I had seen it at a certain distance. 'Oh, but you must see it close to.' Then, turning to an officer, 'Take him and show him our new gun. There is a battery over there. Show him how it works.' And with a gracious wave I was dismissed. As I left the circle I was conscious of a perceptible bristling, almost a murmur among the military potentates who composed it.

When we arrived at the Battery an appreciable parley took place between the Emperor's Aide-de-Camp and the artillery commander. However, before the Imperial insignia every reluctance faded. The gun was displayed. Its breech was opened, and the motions of loading and firing it were gone through by the gunner. I made it evident that I did not wish to pry too closely, and after the usual heel-clicking and saluting we took our departure. There was really nothing for the German officers to worry about. The Emperor knew quite well that I was not an artillery expert, and could learn nothing from a superficial view of his field gun that was not certainly already known by the War Offices of Paris and London. But the impression which he raised in my mind that he was the private proprietor of all these vast and terrific machines, and that he relieved its grim organization with a touch of personal amiability and confidence, was not an unpleasant one.

It was three years before I saw the German Army once more. I was again the guest of the Emperor, and the manoeuvres were this time at Wurzburg, in Bavaria. Many things had changed in the interval. The European outlook had sensibly darkened. The growth of the German Navy had led to the first heavy British counter-measures. The controversy between the British and German Admiralties was sharp. The gradual association of British and French interests was more pronounced. The Young Turk Revolution at Constantinople had set in motion a disturbing train of events in the south-east of Europe. I was now a Member of the Cabinet and President of the Board of Trade—'Handels-Minister' as I was described on my invitation. In 1906 the Emperor had talked to me in great animation and at some length about various Colonial questions, including particularly the native revolt in German South-West Africa. In 1909 I had only one short conversation with him. In this he avoided all military and serious matters, and confined himself to chaff about the Lloyd George Budget and various phases of British domestic politics, with which he showed himself surprisingly well acquainted. This, except for a formal leave-taking, was the last occasion on which I ever spoke to the Emperor, though it was not to be my last contact with the German

Army.

The manoeuvres at Wurzburg showed a great change in German military tactics. A remarkable stride had been made in modernizing their Infantry formations and adapting them to actual war conditions. The absurdities of the Silesian manoeuvres were not repeated. The dense masses were rarely, if ever, seen. The Artillery was not ranged in long lines, but dotted about wherever conveniences of the ground suggested. The whole extent of the battlefield was far greater. The Cavalry were hardly at all in evidence, and then only on distant flanks. The Infantry advanced in successive skirmish lines, and machine-guns everywhere had begun to be a feature. Although these formations were still to British eyes much too dense for modern fire, they nevertheless constituted an enormous advance upon 1906. They were, I believe, substantially the formations with which the German Army five years later entered the Great War, and which were then proved to be superior in efficiency to those of their French opponents.

The next review I saw in Germany was when in 1919 I visited Cologne at the head of the Army Council, and when forty thousand British troops marched past in the solemn glitter of unchallengeable victory. But I did not expect ever to witness such a spectacle when I left Wurzburg in 1909. Indeed no fancy could have seemed more wild.

The reverberations of the Turkish Revolution were already perceptible in the centre of German military life at Wurzburg. Mahmoud Shefket Pasha, the Young-Turkish Minister of War, and Enver Bey were the principal military guests of the German Headquarters. Over both these men hung tragic fates. Shefket was soon to be murdered in Constantinople. Before Enver there stretched a road of toil, of terrorism, of crime, of

disaster which was not to end until his own undaunted
heart and eager frame were stilled for ever. Indeed these
Wurzburg manoeuvres make in my mind the picture of
a Belshazzar feast. Upon how many of those who
marched and cantered in that autumn sunlight had the
dark angel set his seal! Violent untimely death, ruin
and humiliation worse than death, privation, mutilation,
despair to the simple soldier, the downfall of their pride
and subsistence to the chiefs; such were the fates—could
we but have read them—which brooded over thousands
and tens of thousands of these virile figures. All the
Kings and Princes of Germany, all the Generals of her
Empire, clustered round the banqueting-tables. Ten
years were to see them scattered, exiled, deposed, in
penury, in obloquy—the victims of a fatal system in
which they were inextricably involved. And for the
Kaiser, that bright figure, the spoilt child of fortune,
the envy of Europe—for him in the long series of heart-
breaking disappointments and disillusions, of failure and
undying self-reproach, which across the devastation of
Europe was to lead him to the wood-cutter's block at
Doorn—there was surely reserved the sternest punish-
ment of all.

One final incident remains in my mind. I made the
acquaintance of Enver. I was attracted by this fine-
looking young officer, whose audacious gesture had at
the peril of his life swept away the decayed regime of
Abdul Hamid, and who had become in one leopard-
spring the hero of the Turkish nation and the probable
master of its destinies. He evinced a desire to talk about
the Bagdad Railway, with certain aspects of which my
Department was specially concerned, and with which
question as a Minister I was of course closely acquainted.
No opportunity presented itself for this conversation
until the last day of the manoeuvres, when we rode

together alone for an hour amid the thunder of the closing cannonade. We were deep in our subject, and discussing it from an angle not entirely in accord with German views, when we noticed that the horse of the Royal Equerry, who rode behind us, was causing his rider continuous trouble. Four separate times did this animal apparently escape from control, and each time its bounds and curvets carried our attendant close up to us, either between us or alongside, in which position after apologizing for his clumsiness he remained until actually directed to fall back. Over the face of the young Turkish leader, and newly-triumphant conspirator, there played a smile of frank and perfect comprehension. There was no need for us to exchange suspicions.

Had it been possible for the main lines of British policy to have been more in accord with legitimate Turkish aspirations, I am sure we could have worked agreeably with Enver Bey. But all the puppets in the world tragedy were held too tightly in the grip of destiny. Events moved forward remorseless to the supreme catastrophe.

Thoughts and Adventures

Defeat to Germany at sea means nothing but loss of the ships sunk or damaged in battle. Behind the German 'Dreadnoughts' stand four and a half million soldiers and a narrow sea-front bristling with fortresses and batteries. Nothing we could do, after a naval victory, could effect the safety or freedom of a single German hamlet.

Commons, March 17, 1914

If you want a true picture in your mind of a battle between great modern ironclad ships, you must not think of it as if it were two men in armour striking at each other with heavy swords. It is more like a battle

between two eggshells striking each other with hammers.
Speech on the Navy Estimates, 1914

It was the fateful weakness of the German Empire that its military leaders, who knew every detail of their profession and nothing outside it, considered themselves and became arbiters of the whole policy of the State. In France, throughout the war, even in its darkest and most convulsive hours, the civil Government, quivering to its foundations, was nevertheless supreme. . . .

In England Parliament was largely in abeyance . . . But there existed a strong political caste and hierarchy which, if it chose to risk its official existence, could grapple with the 'brass hats'. In the United States, the civil element was so overwhelmingly strong that its main need was to nurture and magnify the unfledged military champions.

Thoughts and Adventures

None should be used until all can be used at once. They should be disposed secretly along the whole attacking front two or three hundred yards apart. Ten or fifteen minutes before the assault these engines should move forward. . . . Nothing but a direct hit from a field-gun will stop them.

If artillery is used to cut wire, the directions and imminence of the attack is proclaimed days beforehand. But by this method the assault follows up the wire-cutting almost immediately, i.e. before any reinforcements can be brought up by the enemy or any special defensive measures taken.

Memo on the use of tanks to Sir John French, C.-in-C., B.E.F., November 1915

Passive defence against such an attack is perfectly

hopeless and endless. You would have to roof in the world to be quite sure. Something may be done, and something has been done by the provision of guns which fire upwards, and by searchlights which train throughout the entire arc, but the only real security upon which sound military principles will rely is that you should be master of your own air.

Commons, March 17, 1914

To have reached the age of forty without ever handling a brush or fiddling with a pencil, to have regarded with mature eye the painting of pictures of any kind as a mystery, to have stood agape before the chalk of the pavement artist, and then suddenly to find oneself plunged in the middle of a new and intense form of interest and action with paints and palettes and canvases, and not to be discouraged by results, is an astonishing and enriching experience. I hope it may be shared by others. I should be glad if these lines induced others to try the experiment which I have tried, and if some at least were to find themselves dowered with an absorbing new amusement delightful to themselves, and at any rate not violently harmful to man or beast.

I hope this is modest enough : because there is no subject on which I feel more humble or yet at the same time more natural. I do not presume to explain how to paint, but only how to get enjoyment. Do not turn the superior eye of critical passivity upon these efforts. Buy a paint-box and have a try. If you need something to occupy your leisure, to divert your mind from the daily round, to illuminate your holidays, do not be too ready to believe that you cannot find what you want here. Even at the advanced age of forty ! It would be a sad pity to shuffle or scramble along through one's playtime with golf and bridge, pottering, loitering, shifting from one heel to the other, wondering what on earth to do—as perhaps is the fate of some unhappy beings—when all the while, if you only knew, there is close at hand a wonderful new world of thought and craft, a sunlit garden gleaming with light and colour of which you have the key in your waistcoat pocket. Inexpensive independence, a mobile and perennial pleasure apparatus, new mental food and exercise, the old harmonies and symmetries in an entirely different language, an added interest to every common scene, an occupation for every idle hour, an unceasing voyage of entrancing discovery—these are high prizes. Make quite sure they are not yours. After all, if you try, and fail, there is not much harm done. The nursery will grab what the studio has rejected. And then you can always go out and kill some animal, humiliate some rival on the links, despoil some friend across the green table. You will not be worse off in any way. In fact you will be better off. You will know 'beyond a peradventure', to quote a phrase disagreeably reminiscent, that that is really what you were meant to do in your hours of relaxation.

But if, on the contrary, you are inclined—late in life though it be—to reconnoitre a foreign sphere of limitless extent, then be persuaded that the first quality that is needed is Audacity. There really is no time for the deliberate approach. Two years of drawing-lessons, three years of copying woodcuts, five years of plaster casts—these are for the young. They have enough to bear. And this thorough grounding is for those who, hearing the call in the morning of their days, are able to make painting their paramount lifelong vocation. The truth and beauty of line and form which by the slightest touch or twist of the brush a real artist imparts to every feature of his design must be founded on long, hard, persevering apprenticeship and a practice so habitual that it has become instinctive. We must not be too ambitious. We cannot aspire to masterpieces. We may content ourselves with a joy ride in a paint-box. And for this Audacity is the only ticket.

I shall now relate my personal experience. When I left the Admiralty at the end of May, 1915, I still remained a member of the Cabinet and of the War Council. In this position I knew everything and could do nothing. The change from the intense executive activities of each day's work at the Admiralty to the narrowly-measured duties of a counsellor left me gasping. Like a sea-beast fished up from the depths, or a diver too suddenly hoisted, my veins threatened to burst from the fall in pressure. I had great anxiety and no means of relieving it; I had vehement convictions and small power to give effect to them. I had to watch the un-happy casting-away of great opportunities, and the feeble execution of plans which I had launched and in which I heartily believed. I had long hours of utterly unwonted leisure in which to contemplate the frightful unfolding of the War. At a moment when every fibre of my being was inflamed to action, I was forced to remain a spectator of the tragedy, placed cruelly in a front seat. And then it was that the Muse of Painting came to my rescue—out of charity and out of chivalry, because after all she had nothing to do with me—and said, 'Are these toys any good to you? They amuse some people.'

Some experiments one Sunday in the country with the children's paint-box led me to procure the next morning a complete outfit for painting in oils.

Having bought the colours, an easel, and a canvas, the next step was to begin. But what a step to take! The palette gleamed with beads of colour; fair and white rose the canvas; the empty brush hung poised, heavy with destiny, irresolute in the air. My hand seemed arrested by a silent veto. But after all the sky on this occasion was unquestionably blue, and a pale blue at that. There could be no doubt that blue paint mixed with white should be put on the top part of the canvas. One really does not need to have had an artist's training to see that. It is a starting-point open to all. So very gingerly I mixed a little blue paint on the palette with a very small brush, and then with infinite precaution made a mark about as big as a bean upon the affronted snow-white shield. It was a challenge, a deliberate challenge; but so subdued, so halting, indeed so cataleptic, that it deserved no response. At that moment the loud approaching sound of a motor-car was heard in the drive. From this chariot there stepped swiftly and lightly none other than the gifted wife of Sir John Lavery. 'Painting! But what are you hesitating about? Let me have a brush—the big one.' Splash into the turpentine, wallop into the blue and the white, frantic flourish on the palette—clean no longer—and then several large fierce strokes and slashes of blue on the absolutely cowering canvas. Anyone could see that it could not hit back. No evil fate avenged the jaunty violence. The canvas grinned in helplessness before me. The spell was broken. The sickly inhibitions rolled away. I seized the largest brush and fell upon my victim with berserk fury. I have never felt any awe of a canvas since.

Everyone knows the feelings with which one stands shivering on a spring-board, the shock when a friendly foe steals up behind and hurls you into the flood, and the ardent glow which thrills you as you emerge breathless from the plunge.

This beginning with Audacity, or being thrown into the middle of it, is already a very great part of the art of painting. But there is more in it than that.

La peinture a l'huile
Est bien difficile,
Mais c'est beaucoup plus beau
Que la peinture a l'eau.

I write no word in disparagement of water-colours. But there really is nothing like oils. You have a medium at your disposal which offers real power, if you only can find out how to use it. Moreover, it is easier to get a certain distance along the road by its means than by water-colour. First of all, you can correct mistakes much more easily. One sweep of the palette-knife 'lifts' the blood and tears of a morning from the canvas and enables a fresh start to be made; indeed the canvas is all the better for past impressions. Secondly, you can approach your problem from any direction. You need not build downwards awkwardly from white paper to your darkest dark. You may strike where you please, beginning if you will with a moderate central arrangement of middle tones, and then hurling in the extremes when the psychological moment comes. Lastly, the pigment itself is such nice stuff to handle (if it does not retaliate). You can build it on layer after layer if you like. You can keep on experimenting. You can change your plan to meet the exigencies of time or weather. And always remember you can scrape it all away.

Just to paint is great fun. The colours are lovely to look at and delicious to squeeze out. Matching them, however crudely, with what you see is fascinating and absolutely absorbing. Try it if you have not done so— before you die. As one slowly begins to escape from the difficulties of choosing the right colours and laying them on in the right places and in the right way, wider considerations come into view. One begins to see, for instance, that painting a picture is like fighting a battle;

and trying to paint a picture is, I suppose, like trying to fight a battle. It is, if anything, more exciting than fighting it successfully. But the principle is the same. It is the same kind of problem, as unfolding a long, sustained, interlocked argument. It is a proposition which, whether of few or numberless parts, is commanded by a single unity of conception. And we think —though I cannot tell—that painting a great picture must require an intellect on the grand scale. There must be that all-embracing view which presents the beginning and the end, the whole and each part, as one instantaneous impression retentively and untiringly held in the mind. When we look at the larger Turners—canvases yards wide and tall—and observe that they are all done in one piece and represent one single second of time, and that every innumerable detail, however small, however distant, however subordinate, is set forth naturally and in its true proportion and relation, without effort, without failure, we must feel in presence of an intellectual manifestation the equal in quality and intensity of the finest achievements of warlike action, or forensic argument, or of scientific or philosophical adjudication.

In all battles two things are usually required of the Commander-in-Chief : to make a good plan for his army and, secondly, to keep a strong reserve. Both these are also obligatory upon the painter. To make a plan, thorough reconnaissance of the country where the battle is to be fought is needed. Its fields, its mountains, its rivers, its bridges, its trees, its flowers, its atmosphere— all require and repay attentive obervation from a special point of view. One is quite astonished to find how many things there are in the landscape, and in every object in it, one never noticed before. And this is a tremendous new pleasure and interest which invests every walk or drive with an added object. So many colours on the hillside, each different in shadow and in sunlight; such brilliant reflections in the pool, each a key lower than what they repeat; such lovely lights gilding or silvering surface or outline, all tinted exquisitely with pale colour, rose, orange, green, or violet. I found myself instinctively as I walked noting the tint and character of a leaf, the dreamy purple shades of mountains, the exquisite lacery of winter branches, the dim pale silhouettes of far horizons. And I had lived for over forty years without ever noticing any of them except in a general way, as one might look at a crowd and say, 'What a lot of people!'

I think this heightened sense of observation of Nature is one of the chief delights that have come to me through trying to paint. No doubt many people who are lovers of art have acquired it in a high degree without actually practising. But I expect that nothing will make one observe more quickly or more thoroughly than having to face the difficulty of representing the thing observed. And mind you, if you do observe accurately and with refinement, and if you do record what you have seen with tolerable correspondence, the result follows on the canvas with startling obedience. Even if only four or five main features are seized and truly recorded, these by themselves will carry a lot of ill-success or half-success. Answer five big questions out of all the hundreds in the examination paper correctly and well, and though you may not win a prize, at any rate you will not be absolutely ploughed.

But in order to make his plan, the General must not only reconnoitre the battle-ground, he must also study the achievements of the great Captains of the past. He must bring the observations he has collected in the field into comparison with the treatment of similar incidents by famous chiefs. Then the galleries of Europe take on a new—and to me at least a severely practical—interest. 'This, then, is how —— painted a cataract. Exactly, and there is that same light I noticed last week in the waterfall at ——' And so on. You see the difficulty that baffled you yesterday; and you see how easily it has been overcome by a great or even by a skilful painter. Not only is your observation of Nature sensibly improved and developed, but you look at the masterpieces of art with an analysing and a comprehending eye.

The whole world is open with all its treasures. The simplest objects have their beauty. Every garden presents innumerable fascinating problems. Every land, every parish, has its own tale to tell. And there are many lands differing from each other in countless ways, and each presenting delicious variants of colour, light, form, and definition. Obviously, then, armed with a paint-box one cannot be bored, one cannot be left at a loose end, one cannot 'have several days on one's hands'. Good gracious! what there is to admire and how little time there is to see it in! For the first time one begins to envy Methuselah. No doubt he made a very indifferent use of his opportunities.

But it is in the use and withholding of their reserves that the great commanders have generally excelled. After all, when once the last reserve has been thrown in, the commander's part is played. If that does not win the battle, he has nothing else to give. The event must be left to luck and to the fighting troops. But these last, in the absence of high direction, are apt to get into sad confusion, all mixed together in a nasty mess, without order or plan—and consequently without effect. Mere masses count no more. The largest brush, the brightest colours cannot even make an impression. The pictorial battlefield becomes a sea of mud mercifully veiled by the fog of war. It is evident there has been a serious defeat.

Even though the General plunges in himself and emerges bespattered, as he sometimes does, he will not retrieve the day.

In painting, the reserves consist in Proportion or Relation. And it is here that the art of the painter marches along the road which is traversed by all the greatest harmonies in thought. At one side of the palette there is white, at the other black; and neither is ever used 'neat'. Between these two rigid limits all the action must lie, all the power required must be generated. Black and white themselves placed in juxtaposition make no great impression; and yet they are the most that you can do in pure contrast. It is wonderful—after one has tried and failed often—to see how easily and surely the true artist is able to produce every effect of light and shade, of sunshine and shadow, of distance or nearness, simply by expressing justly the relations between the different planes and surfaces with which he is dealing. We think that this is founded upon a sense of proportion, trained no doubt by practice, but which in its essence is a frigid manifestation of mental power and size. We think that the same mind's eye that can justly survey and appraise and prescribe beforehand the values of a truly great picture in one all-embracing regard, in one flash of simultaneous and homogeneous comprehension, would also with a certain acquaintance with the special technique be able to pronounce with sureness upon any other high activity of the human intellect. This was certainly true of the great Italians.

I have written in this way to show how varied are the delights which may be gained by those who enter hopefully and thoughtfully upon the pathway of painting; how enriched they will be in their daily vision, how fortified in their independence, how happy in their leisure. Whether you feel that your soul is pleased by the conception or contemplation of harmonies, or that your mind is stimulated by the aspect of magnificent problems, or whether you are content to find fun in trying to observe and depict the jolly things you see, the vistas of possibility are limited only by the shortness of life. Every day you may make progress. Every step may be fruitful. Yet there will stretch out before you an ever-lengthening, ever-ascending, ever-improving path. You know you will never get to the end of the journey. But this, so far from discouraging, only adds to the joy and glory of the climb.

Try it, then, before it is too late and before you mock at me. Try it while there is time to overcome the preliminary difficulties. Learn enough of the language in your prime to open this new literature to your age. Plant a garden in which you can sit when digging days are done. It may be only a small garden, but you will see it grow. Year by year it will bloom and ripen. Year by year it will be better cultivated. The weeds will be cast out. The fruit-trees will be pruned and trained. The flowers will bloom in more beautiful combinations. There will be sunshine there even in the winter-time and cool shade, and the play of shadow on the pathway in the shining days of June.

I must say I like bright colours. I agree with Ruskin in his denunciation of that school of painting who 'eat slate-pencil and chalk, and assure everybody that they are nicer and purer than strawberries and plums'. I cannot pretend to feel impartial about the colours. I rejoice with the brilliant ones, and am genuinely sorry for the poor browns. When I get to heaven I mean to spend a considerable portion of my first million years in painting, and so get to the bottom of the subject. But then I shall require a still gayer palette than I get here below. I expect orange and vermilion will be the

97

darkest, dullest colours upon it, and beyond them there will be a whole range of wonderful new colours which will delight the celestial eye.

Chance led me one autumn to a secluded nook on the Côte d'Azur, between Marseilles and Toulon, and there I fell in with one or two painters who revelled in the methods of the modern French school. These were disciples of Cézanne. They view Nature as a mass of shimmering light in which forms and surfaces are comparatively unimportant, indeed, hardly visible, but which gleams and glows with beautiful harmonies and contrasts of colour. Certainly it was of great interest to me to come suddenly in contact with this entirely different way of looking at things. I had hitherto painted the sea flat, with long, smooth strokes of mixed pigment in which the tints varied only by gradations. Now I must try to represent it by innumerable small separate lozenge-shaped points and patches of colour—often pure colour—so that it looked more like a tessellated pavement than a marine picture. It sounds curious. All the same, do not be in a hurry to reject the method. Go back a few yards and survey the result. Each of these little points of colour is now playing his part in the general effect. Individually invisible, he sets up a strong radiation, of which the eye is conscious without detecting the cause. Look also at the blue of the Mediterranean. How can you depict and record it? Certainly not by any single colour that was ever manufactured. The only way in which the luminous intensity of blue can be simulated is by this multitude of tiny points of varied colour all in true relation to the rest of the scheme. Difficult? Fascinating!

Nature presents itself to the eye through the agency of these individual points of light, each of which sets up the vibrations peculiar to its colour. The brilliancy of a picture must therefore depend partly upon the frequency with which these points are found on any given area of the canvas, and partly on their just relation to one another. Ruskin says in his *Elements of Drawing,* from which I have already quoted, 'You will not, in Turner's largest oil pictures, perhaps six or seven feet long by four or five high, find one spot of colour as large as a grain of wheat ungradated.' But the gradations of Turner differ from those of the modern French school by being gently and almost imperceptibly evolved one from another instead of being bodily and even roughly separated; and the brush of Turner followed the form of he objects he depicted, while our French friends often seem to take a pride in directly opposing it. For instance, they would prefer to paint a sea with up and down strokes rather than with horizontal; or a tree-trunk from right to left rather than up and down. This, I expect, is due to falling in love with one's theories, and making sacrifices of truth to them in order to demonstrate fidelity and admiration.

But surely we owe a debt to those who have so wonderfully vivified, brightened, and illuminated modern landscape painting. Have not Manet and Monet, Cezanne and Matisse, rendered to painting something of the same service which Keats and Shelley gave to poetry after the solemn and ceremonious literary perfections of the eighteenth century? They have brought back to the pictorial art a new draught of joie de vivre; and the beauty of their work is instinct with gaiety, and floats in sparkling air.

I do not expect these masters would particularly appreciate my defence, but I must avow an increasing attraction to their work. Lucid and exact expression is one of the characteristics of the French mind. The French language has been made the instrument of the admirable gift. Frenchmen talk and write just as well about painting as they have done about love, about war, about diplomacy, or cooking. Their terminology is precise and complete. They are therefore admirably equipped to be teachers in the theory of any of these arts. Their critical faculty is so powerfully developed that it is perhaps some restraint upon achievement. But it is a wonderful corrective to others as well as to themselves.

My French friend, for instance, after looking at some of my daubs, took me round the galleries of Paris, pausing here and there. Wherever he paused, I found myself before a picture which I particularly admired. He then explained that it was quite easy to tell, from the kind of things I had been trying to do, what were the things I liked. Never having taken any interest in pictures till I tried to paint, I had no preconceived opinions. I just felt, for reasons I could not fathom, that I liked some much more than others. I was astonished that anyone else should, on the most cursory observation of my work, be able so surely to divine a taste which I had never consciously formed. My friend said that it is not a bad thing to know nothing at all about pictures, but to have a matured mind trained in other things and a new strong interest in painting. The elements are there from which a true taste in art can be formed with time and guidance, and there are no obstacles or imperfect conceptions in the way. I hope this is true. Certainly the last part is true.

Once you begin to study it, all Nature is equally interesting and equally charged with beauty. I was shown a picture by Cezanne of a blank wall of a house, which he had made instinct with the most delicate lights and colours. Now I often amuse myself when I am looking at a wall or a flat surface of any kind by trying to distinguish all the different colours and tints which can be discerned upon it, and considering whether these arise from reflections or from natural hue. You would be astonished the first time you tried this to see how many and what beautiful colours there are even in the most commonplace objects, and the more carefully and frequently you look the more variations do you perceive.

But these are no reasons for limiting oneself to the plainest and most ordinary objects and scenes. Mere prettiness of scene, to be sure, is not needed for a beautiful picture. In fact, artificially-made pretty places are very often a hindrance to a good picture. Nature will hardly stand a double process of beautification : one layer of idealism on top of another is too much of a good thing. But a vivid scene, a brilliant atmosphere, novel and charming lights, impressive contrasts, if they strike the eye all at once, arouse an interest and an ardour which will certainly be reflected in the work which you try to do, and will make it seem easier.

It would be interesting if some real authority investigated carefully the part which memory plays in painting. We look at the object with an intent regard, then at the palette, and thirdly at the canvas. The canvas receives a message dispatched usually a few seconds before from the natural object. But it has come though a post-office en route. It has been transmitted in code. It has been turned from light into paint. It reaches the canvas a cryptogram. Not until it has been placed in its correct relation to everything else that is on the canvas can it be deciphered, is its meaning apparent, is it translated once again from mere pigment into light. And the light this time is not of Nature but of Art. The whole of this considerable process is carried through on the wings or the wheels of memory. In most cases we think it is the wings—airy and quick like a butterfly from flower to flower. But all heavy traffic and all that has to go a long journey must travel on wheels.

In painting in the open air the sequence of actions is so rapid that the process of translation into and out of pigment may seem to be unconscious. But all the greatest landscapes have been painted indoors, and often long after the first impressions were gathered. In a dim cellar the Dutch or Italian master recreated the gleaming ice of a Netherlands carnival or the lustrous sunshine of Venice or the Campagna. Here, then, is required a formidable memory of the visual kind. Not only do we develop our powers of observation, but also those of carrying the record—of carrying it through an extraneous medium and of reproducing it, hours, days, or even months after the scene has vanished or the sunlight died.

It was told by a friend that when Whistler guided a school in Paris he made his pupils observe their model on the ground floor, and then run upstairs and paint their picture piece by piece on the floor above. As they became more proficient he put their easels up a storey higher, till at last the elite were scampering with their decision up six flights into the attic—praying it would not evaporate on the way. This is, perhaps, only a tale. But it shows effectively of what enormous importance a trained, accurate, retentive memory must be to an artist; and conversely what a useful exercise painting may be for the development of an accurate and retentive memory.

There is no better exercise for the would-be artist than to study and devour a picture, and then, without looking at it again, to attempt the next day to reproduce it. Nothing can more exactly measure the progress both of observation and memory. It is still harder to compose out of many separate, well-retained impressions, aided though they be by sketches and colour notes, a new complete conception. But this is the only way in which great landscapes have been painted—or can be painted. The size of the canvas alone precludes its being handled out of doors. The fleeting light imposes a rigid time-limit. The same light never returns. One cannot go back day after day without the picture getting stale. The painter must choose between a rapid impression, fresh and warm and living, but probably deserving only of a short life, and the cold, profound, intense effort of memory, knowledge, and will-power, prolonged perhaps for weeks, from which a master-piece can alone result. It is much better not to fret too much about the latter. Leave to the masters of art trained by a lifetime of devotion the wonderful process of picture-building and picture-creation. Go out into the sunlight and be happy with what you see.

Painting is complete as a distraction. I know of nothing which, without exhausting the body, more entirely absorbs the mind. Whatever the worries of the hour or the threats of the future, once the picture has begun to flow along, there is no room for them in the mental screen. They pass out into shadow and darkness. All one's mental light, such as it is, becomes concentrated on the task. Time stands respectfully aside, and it is only after many hesitations that luncheon knocks gruffly at the door. When I have had to stand up on parade, or even, I regret to say, in church, for half an hour at a time, I have always felt that the erect position is not natural to man, has only been painfully acquired, and is only with fatigue and difficulty maintained. But no one who is fond of painting finds the slightest inconvenience, as long as the interest holds, in standing to paint for three or four hours at a stretch.

Lastly, let me say a word on painting as a spur to

travel. There is really nothing like it. Every day and all day is provided with its expedition and its occupation— cheap, attainable, innocent, absorbing, recuperative. The vain racket of the tourist gives place to the calm enjoyment of the philosopher, intensified by an enthralling sense of action and endeavour. Every country where the sun shines and every district in it has a theme of its own. The lights, the atmosphere, the aspect, the spirit, are all different; but each has its native charm. Even if you are only a poor painter you can feel the influence of the scene, guiding your brush, selecting the tubes you squeeze on to the palette. Even if you cannot portray it as you see it, you feel it, you know it, and you admire it for ever. When people rush about Europe in the train from one glittering centre of work or pleasure to another, passing—at enormous expense—through a series of mammoth hotels and blatant carnivals, they little know what they are missing, and how cheaply priceless things can be obtained. The painter wanders and loiters contentedly from place to place, always on the look out for some brilliant butterfly of a picture which can be caught and set up and carried safely home.

Now I am learning to like painting even on dull days. But in my hot youth I demanded sunshine. Sir William Orpen advised me to visit Avignon on account of its wonderful light, and certainly there is no more delightful centre for a would-be painter's activities: then Egypt, fierce and brilliant, presenting in infinite variety the single triplex theme of the Nile, the desert, and the sun; or Palestine, a land of rare beauty—the beauty of the turquoise and the opal—which well deserves the attention of some real artist, and has never been portrayed to the extent that is its due. And what of India? Who has ever interpreted its lucid splendours? But after all, if only the sun will shine, one does not need to go beyond one's own country. There is nothing more intense than the burnished steel and gold of a Highland stream; and at the beginning and close of almost every day the Thames displays to the citizens of London glories and delights which one must travel far to rival.

Thoughts and Adventures

I did not see Lawrence again for some weeks. It was, if my memory serves me right, in Paris. He wore his Arab robes, and the full magnificence of his countenance revealed itself. The gravity of his demeanour; the precision of his opinions; the range and quality of his conversation; all seemed enhanced to a remarkable degree by the splendid Arab head-dress and garb. From amid the flowing draperies his noble features, his perfectly-chiselled lips and flashing eyes loaded with fire and comprehension shone forth. He looked what he was, one of Nature's greatest princes. We got on much better this time, and I began to form that impression of his strength and quality which since has never left me. Whether he wore the prosaic clothes of English daily life or afterwards in the uniform of an Air Force mechanic, I always saw him henceforward as he appears in Augustus John's brilliant pencil sketch.

Great Contemporaries

Over a long period of years the peace and order of the British Empire was, in fact, maintained by about seventy-five battalions abroad and seventy-five at home, with the due proportion of the other arms. Is it not a wonder and is it not an admirable fact, that the Imperial authority should have been maintained over these vast expanses comprising more than one-fifth, I believe, of the entire population of the world by less than a quarter of a million of white soldiers? To find a parallel you have to go back to the greatest period of the Roman Empire, to the age of the Antonines; to find a parallel for so great and so wide a peace being sustained upon so slender an armed force you have to go back to the Antonines, and even then the parallel is greatly in favour of the British example.

Commons, February 23, 1920

Might not a bomb no bigger than an orange be found to possess a secret power to destroy a whole street of buildings—nay, to concentrate the force of a thousand tons of cordite and blast a township at a stroke? Could not explosives even of the existing type be guided automatically in flying machines by wireless or other rays, without a human pilot, in ceaseless procession upon a hostile city, arsenal, camp, or dockyard?

Thoughts and Adventures, 1925

If the Viceroys and Governments of India in the past had given half as much attention to dealing with the social conditions of the masses of the Indian people as they have to busying themselves with negotiating with unrepresentative leaders of the political classes for constitutional changes—if they had addressed themselves to the moral and material problems which are at the root of Indian life, I think it would have been much better for the working folk of Burnley and Bombay, of Oldham and Ahmadabad.

Speech in the House, July 9, 1931

France, though armed to the teeth, is pacifist to the core.

Speech in the House of Commons, November 23, 1932

You talk of secret diplomacy, but let me tell you that there is a worse kind of secret diplomacy, and it is the diplomacy which spreads out hope and soothing-syrup for the good, while all the time winks are exchanged between the people who know actually what is going on.

Commons, March 14, 1933

Stripped of her Empire in the Orient, deprived of the sovereignty of the seas, loaded with debt and taxation, her commerce and carrying trade shut out by foreign tariffs and quotas, England would sink to the level of a fifth-rate Power and nothing would remain of all her glories except a population much larger than this island can support.

Speech to the Royal Society of St. George, April 24, 1933

Even taking the lowest view of human nature, nations in war do not usually do things which give them no special advantage, and which grievously complicate their own position.

Commons, March 8, 1934

It is a mistake to suppose that the problem of averting another European or probably a world war depends to any important extent either upon the reply which Herr Hitler has made to the Locarno Powers, or to staff conversations now decided upon betwen Great Britain and France or Belgium. Herr Hitler is continuing his efforts to separate Great Britain from France, and also to separate British public opinion from the British Government and House of Commons. The British Government, on the other hand, is anxious to comfort France in view of the great restraint which France, largely in deference to British wishes, has observed in presence of the German breach of treaties and military reoccupation of the Rhine zone. The realities are far larger and more profound than either of these moves upon the diplomatic chessboard.

First stands the rapid and tremendous rearmament of Germany, which is proceeding night and day and is steadily converting nearly seventy millions of the most efficient race in Europe into one gigantic, hungry war-machine. The second is that the recent actions of Germany have destroyed all confidence in her respect for treaties, whether imposed as the result of defeat in war or freely entered into by post-war Germany and confirmed by the Nazi regime. The third is that practically the whole of the German nation has been taught to regard the incorporation in the Reich of the Germanic population of neighbouring states as a natural, rightful and inevitable aim of Germany policy. The fourth is that the financial and economic pressures in Germany are rising to such a pitch that Herr Hitler's government will in a comparatively short time have only to choose between an internal and an external explosion.

Anyone who bears these terrible and sombre realities constantly in mind will acquire that sense of proportion without which the daily gestures and speeches of rulers, politicians and diplomatists are liable to be merely misleading. All who have acquired this indispensable standard of judgment will see that the issue which is open is not really one between Germany and France, nor between Germany and the Locarno Powers. It is an issue between Germany and the League of Nations. Indeed, expressed in its most searching terms, it is a life and death struggle between the Nazi regime in Germany and the principles of the Covenant of the League of Nations reiterated by the Kellogg Pact.

It therefore concerns all nations, including the German people themselves : but it concerns them all in very different degrees. The countries which lie upon or near the borders of Germany are in the front line. They see the wonderful roads along which four columns of troops or motor vhicles can move abreast, brought to their own frontier terminals. They dwell under the flickering shadow of the most fearful sword ever wrought by human agency, now uplifted in flashing menace, now held anew to the grindstone. Those that are more remote from the German arsenals and training centres have naturally a greater sense of detachment. But none, even though protected by the oceans can, as experience of the last war proved, afford to view with indifference the processes which are already in motion.

The dear desire of all the peoples, not perhaps even excluding a substantial portion of the German people themselves, is to avoid another horrible war in which their lives and homes will be destroyed or ruined and such civilisation as we have been able to achieve reduced to primordial pulp and squalor. Never till now were great communities afforded such ample means of measuring their approaching agony. Never have they seemed less capable of taking effective measures to prevent it. Chattering, busy, sporting, toiling, amused from day to day by headlines and from night to night by cinemas, they yet can feel themselves slipping, sinking, rolling backward to the age when 'the earth was void and darkness moved upon the face of the waters'. Surely it is worth a supreme effort—the laying aside of every impediment, the clear-eyed facing of fundamental facts, the noble acceptance of risks inseparable from heroic endeavour—to control the hideous drift of events and arrest calamity upon the threshold. Stop it! Stop it!! Stop it now!!! now is the appointed time.

When, on that Friday night three weeks ago, Herr Hitler, against the advice of his generals, ordered his redoubtable troops to march through the 'scraps of paper' to occupy and entrench the Rhineland, he set in motion a trend of events which offered nothing less than blessing or cursing to mankind. Which fate shall befall us rests no longer with him, but with the world. The world, nay, Europe alone, is overwhelmingly strong compared to any single member of its family. But there must be Concert and Design guided by farsighted unselfishness and sustained by inexorable resolve. This is no task for France; no task for Britain; no task for the Locarno Powers or any group of Powers; no task for small Powers nor for great; it is a task for all. The means are at hand; the occasion has come. There may still be time.

Let the States and peoples who lie in fear of Germany carry their alarms to the League of Nations at Geneva. Let the greatest among them lead the way and marshal the assembly. Let none be a laggard or a doubter. Let the League, if satisfied that their fears are well-founded, authorise, nay, adjure them, to take forthwith all necessary measures for mutual protection, and require them to stand in readiness alike to submit themselves to, or, if need be, enforce the reign of international law. Let us have, in the words of a writer in *The Times*: 'A block of peaceable and resolute nations determined to make a stand against aggression in any form.' Let the League then address Germany collectively, not only upon her treaty breaches but also upon her own grievances and anxieties, and, above all, upon her armaments. Let Germany receive from united nations a guarantee of the inviolability of her own soil unless she invades the soil of others. Let unchallengeable power and fair play march hand in hand. Let us move forward by measured steps, without haste and without rest, to a faithful and a lasting settlement in accordance with the general need.

Newspaper article of April 3, 1936

From being the least vulnerable of all nations we have through developments in the air, become the most vulnerable.

Commons, March 19, 1935

It is very much better sometimes to have a panic feeling beforehand, and then be quite calm when things happen, than to be extremely calm beforehand and to get into a panic when things happen.

Speech in the House, May 22, 1935

We live in such a febrile and sensational age, that even a month or two is enough to make people not merely change their views, but to forget the views and feeling they entertained before.

Commons, October 24, 1935

Should Germany at any time make war in Europe, we may be sure that Japan will immediately light a second conflagration in the Far East.

From a letter, November 27, 1936

When I first went into Parliament, now nearly forty years ago . . . the most insulting charge which could be made against a Minister . . . short of actual malfeasance, was that he had endangered the safety of the country . . . for electioneering considerations. Yet such are the surprising qualities of Mr. Baldwin that what all had been taught to shun has now been elevated into a canon of political virtue.

Letter, December 11, 1936

Moral force, is unhappily, no substitute for armed force, but it is a very great reinforcement.

Speech in the House, December 21, 1937

We have never been likely to get into trouble by having an extra thousand or two of up-to-date aeroplanes at our disposal. . . . As the man whose mother-in-law had died in Brazil replied, when asked how the remains should be disposed of : "Embalm, cremate, and bury. Take no risks!"

From an article on world affairs, April 28, 1938

What is this Covenant by which we are to stand? It is the Covenant of the League of Nations. After the calamities of the Great War, many States and people banded themselves together to establish a system of collective security, whereby the violent aggression of one Government upon another should be curbed and prevented; and so that processes should be devised whereby the grievances of peoples or communities should be redressed fairly and sincerely without recourse to war. By the Covenant of the League, and by the Kellogg Pact, almost all countries have bound themselves to adopt these principles, to enforce them, and to submit themselves to them.

How far, alas, do man's endeavours fall short in practice of his inspirations! Great States and peoples have fallen away. Some have violated the faith they had pledged. Some are seduced by intrigue, or have yielded themselves to the cynical, short-sighted and selfish. Many are oppressed by a sense of isolation and weakness. Others are obviously frightened. The Covenant has been broken. The League has been frustrated. Over all the anxious Governments, over all the vast masses, broods the baleful shadow of disunity and failure. In our ears ring the taunts of mockery and the reproach of fiasco . . .

It is said that the League will embroil us in other peoples' quarrels, and we shall get no corrersponding protection in return. Let us examine that objection. We are already deeply involved in Europe. Only a month ago the Prime Minister read out to the House of Commons a long list of countries in whose defence we were bound to go to war : France, Belgium, Portugal, Egypt and Iraq. He then discussed another class of countries which might become the victims of aggression, for whom we were not bound to go to war, but whose fate was a matter of great interest to us. We would not make any automatic and obligatory commitments in regard to them, but would judge an act of aggression when it occurred. Take the case of Czechoslovakia which he mentioned. Although we have not gone as far as France in giving a pledge to Czechoslovakia, Mr. Chamberlain has gone a long way. We are the ally of France which would certainly be involved. We may be drawn in, says the Prime Minister, by the force of circumstances, even in cases where there is no legal engagement. Finally we are at this minute offering advice to Czechoslovakia, and if she takes that advice, and makes the concessions we think right, and finds herself attacked none the less, is it not clear that we are morally entangled? We have thus in this case, the most urgent, undertaken in the name of detachment, engagements beyond what the Covenant prescribes. The Covenant does not prescribe that we should go to war for Czechoslovakia, or any other country, but only that we should not be neutral in the sense of being indifferent as between an aggressor and the victim of aggression.

If the war breaks out in Europe, no one can say how far it will spread, or who will have it in their power to stand out of it. Is it not better then, on grounds of prudence alone, to gain the strength which comes from combined action? Is it not wise to try to invest the Covenant with reality, to unite as many nations as possible in its support, to gain a measure of protection for ourselves, in return for the risks we are to run for others. By this present policy of decrying the League and making the Covenant a matter of division between parties we are only having the disadvantage of both courses. It would indeed be disastrous if we were led into a fierce division here at home about foreign policy. An election fought on ordinary domestic issues is a process with which we are all familiar; but an election turning on the dread issues of defence and foreign policy might leave us a deeply divided nation, with an evenly balanced, incoherent Parliament, and this at the very moment when the danger on the Continent had reached its height. That is why I plead for national unity, and for a policy upon which alone it is to be achieved. We might be having a general election in this country, or preparing for one, with both sides rivalling each other as to who was most in favour of peace at any price. We might have this at the very moment when the warlust of dictator Powers had reached its culminating explosion point.

But we are told that we must not involve ourselves in a quarrel about ideologies. If this means that we are not to back Communism against Nazi-ism or vice versa, we all agree. Both doctrines are equally obnoxious to the principles of freedom. Certainly we should not back one against the other. But surely we must have an opinion between Right and Wrong? Surely we must have an opinion between Aggressor and Victim? This is no question of resisting dictators because they are dictators, but only if they attack other people. Have we not an ideology—if we must use this ugly word—of our own in freedom, in a liberal constitution, in democratic and parliamentary government, in Magna Charta and the Petition of Rights? Ought we not to be ready to make as many sacrifices and exertions for our own broad central theme and cause, as the fanatics of either of these new creeds? Ought we not to produce in defence of Right, champions as bold, missionaries as eager, and if need be, swords as sharp as are at the disposal of the leaders of totalitarian States?

Finally, there must be a moral basis for British foreign policy. People in this country, after all we have gone through, do not mean to be drawn into another terrible war in the name of old-world alliances or diplomatic combinations. If deep causes of division are to be removed from our midst, if all our energies are to be concentrated upon the essential task of increasing our strength and security, it can only be because of lofty and unselfish ideals which command the allegiance of all classes here at home, which rouse their echoes in the breasts even of the dictator-ridden peoples, themselves, and stir the pulses of the English-speaking race in every quarter of the globe. That is why I say 'Stand by the Covenant and endeavour to revive and fortify the strength of the League'.

Here is the practical plan. Britain and France are now united. Together they are an enormous force moral and physical, and one which few would dare to challenge. I should like to see these two countries go to all the smaller States that are menaced, who are going to be devoured one by one by the Nazi tyranny, and say to them bluntly, 'We are not going to help you if you are not going to help yourselves. What are you going to do about it? What are you going to contribute? Are you prepared to take special service in defence of the Covenant? If you are willing to do so, and to prove it by actions, then we will join together with you, if there are enough of you, in active military association under the authority of the League in order to protect each other and the world from another act of aggression.'

You cannot expect all the States of the League to take equal obligations. Some are far away and some are in no danger. But if we could rally even ten well-armed States in Europe, all banded together to resist an aggression upon any one of them, all banded together to counter-attack the aggressor upon a combined plan, then we should be so strong that the immediate danger would be warded off, and a breathing space be gained for building a still broader structure of peace. Is that not far better than being dragged piecemeal into a war when half those who might have been your friends and allies will have already been pulled down one by one? No single nation should be asked to enter into this solemn engagement unless it is assured of strong and valiant comrades banded together not only by a covenant of high ideals, but by practical military conventions. In this way we have the best chance of preventing a war, and if that fails, of surviving it unconquered.

But even that would only be a beginning. To the east of Europe lies the enormous power of Russia, a country whose form of government I detest, but which at any rate seeks no military aggression upon its neighbours, a country whose interests are peace, a country profoundly menaced by Nazi hostility, a country which lies as a great background and counterpoise at this moment to all those States of Middle Europe I have mentioned. We should certainly not go cap in hand to Soviet Russia, or count in any definite manner upon Russian action. But how improvidently foolish we should be when dangers are so great, to put needless barriers in the way of the general association of the great Russian mass with resistance to an act of Nazi aggression.

There is, however, a third stage in the process. There is Poland; and the countries of the north, the Baltic States, the Scandinavian Powers. If we had once gathered together the forces I have mentioned, we should then be in a position to offer these countries a very great measure of armed security for peace. At the present time they do not know which way to turn. But if they saw a strong, armed association, such as I have described, whose interest in peace was the same as theirs, they might easily be induced to throw in their lot with us and 'make assurance double sure'.

But what is this but a recreated League of Nations, devoted to its original purpose, namely the prevention of war? If we could, therefore, get as far as this, believe me the war danger would be removed from us perhaps for our lifetime. And across the Atlantic Ocean the United States would signal her encouragement and sympathy.

I shall be told, 'But this is the encirclement of Germany.' I say, 'No, this is the encirclement of an aggressor.' Nations who are bound by the Covenant can never, however powerful they may be, menace the peace and independence of any other State. That is the essence of the conditions which bring them together. To form a war combination against a single State would be a crime. To form a combination for mutual defence against a probable aggressor is not only no crime, but the highest moral duty and virtue. We ask no security for ourselves that we are not prepared freely to extend to Germany. If Germany nourishes no aggressive designs, if Germany professes herself to be afraid of attack, let her join too; let her join the club and share fairly and equally all its privileges and safeguards.

Now, that is a foreign policy which involves us in no

commitments more entangling than those which we have already taken, and which gives us the possibilities should it be successful—and one can but try—of substantial if not absolute security. There is nothing visionary or sentimental about such a policy. It is nothing more nor less than common sense, and in addition it is enshrined in that great structure of international law and unity embodied in the League of Nations and the Covenant. This may be a noble dream, but it is also a practical plan, and one which I believe, if pursued with courage, comprehension and decision, would rally a peaceful Europe around a strong Britain and France. It is not even now too late to carry such a policy through to success. Then when we have gathered these forces, and by united strength removed the fear of war, then will be the time to deal with the grievances of discontented nations, to get rid of the causes of hatred and jealousy, as you will have removed the causes of fear. Then will be the time to proceed to the culmination of the whole work, namely, the broad general reduction of the hideous burden of armaments, which if it continues to grow at its present rate can only lead through bankruptcy to mutual destruction.

Before you reject this great hope with all its effort and its risk, which I in no wise conceal, consider the alternative. There is another foreign policy which you are urged to pursue. It is not to worry about all these countries of Central Europe, not to trouble yourself with preserving the Covenant of the League, to recognize that all that is foolish and vain and can never be restored, and to make a special pact of friendship with Nazi Germany. There is no reason why we should not live in a friendly manner with Germany. It is our duty to try to do so, little as we like her system of government, deeply as we are revolted by the cruel racial and religious persecution on which the flames of Nazi hatred feed themselves. Still, in making an international arrangement to preserve the peace of the world, we could no more exclude Nazi Germany than Soviet Russia. But when we are told we must make a special pact with Nazi Germany, I want to know what that pact is going to be, and at whose expense it is to be made. Undoubtedly our Government could make an agreement with Germany. All they have to do is to give her back her former colonies and such others as she may desire; to muzzle the British Press and platform by a law of censorship, and to give Herr Hitler a free hand to spread the Nazi system and dominance far and wide through Central Europe. That is the alternative foreign policy. It is one which, in my view, would be disgraceful and disastrous. In the first place it leads us straight to war. The Nazi regime, elated by this triumph, with every restraint removed, would proceed unchecked upon its path of ambition and aggression. We should be the helpless, silent, gagged, apparently consenting, spectators of the horrorrs which would spread through Central Europe. The Government that enforced such a policy would be swept away. The mere instinct of self-preservation would make it impossible for us to purchase a fleeting and precarious immunity at the cost of the ruin and enslavement of Europe. After an interval, long or short, we should be drawn into a war, like the United States were drawn into the Great War. But by that time we should be confronted with an antagonist, overwhelmingly powerful, and find ourselves deprived of every friend.

Have I not set out to you these issues plainly? And is there any doubt which way duty and safety point? Hitherto I have been dealing with questions about which there is confusion of thought in our country, and about which there may be a grievous division at a time when unity is vital. But now I come to an issue upon which we are all agreed, namely the rearmament of our country for its own security, to discharge its duties, and to maintain its safety. There is a need for greater effort. There is a need for united effort. There is a need to lay aside our easy-going life, to have efficiency and a broad national plan.

A large part of our dangers and the dangers of Europe is due to the fact that we did not rearm in time. It was certainly not through lack of warning, but when we at last began it was only in a half-hearted, ramshackle, confused manner which, though it has led to great outpourings of money, has not been attended by proportionate results. Is it not lamentable that our Air Force is not now fully equal to any Power within striking distance of these shores? Is it not grievous that the vast, flexible industry of Britain has not yet been able to produce a broad and copious flow of the latest weapons of all kinds? After all, it is nearly three years since Mr. Baldwin recognized the dangers which beset us. Late as we started we ought by now to be in a strong position. Parliament is to discuss this matter this week. There ought certainly to be a searching inquiry into the condition of the Air Force, and into the reasons why the solemn pledge given to the country by Mr. Baldwin of air parity has been broken.

But an equal confusion and delay covers large parts of the field of munitions supply. It is greatly to be regretted that after nearly three years since the Government became alive to the dangers, and nearly five years since the danger became apparent, the equipment of our small Regular Army should be incomplete, and that the supplying of the Territorial Army with modern weapons and appliances should be only in a rudimentary stage. As for Air Raid Precautions, artillery, balloons, organization in every form, you know for yourselves—as well as the Germans know—the unhappy and discreditable conditions which prevail. This is no case for the Opposition to make party capital against the Government. Nor for the Government to try to shield incompetence and misdirection. All should set country before party. There should be a thorough and searching inquest into the mismanagement of the past and a fearless resolve to sweep away every obstacle that stands in the path of our regaining our national safety. Meanwhile everyone must do his best.

Look at the danger in which we stand. Germany has been rearming night and day for four years. For four years past they have never spent less in any year than £300,000,000 sterling on war preparation. The whole manhood of the country is harnessed to war. Even the children are organized. Every thought is turned to race assertion and the conquest of weaker, more exhausted, or less determined breeds. They are driving forward on their path. Every six weeks a new army corps is added to their active forces. Never has there been such an outpouring of munitions of war. At present we are shielded to some extent by the strength of the French army, but the German numbers are overtaking them month by month. We have still our Navy, never, happily, so supreme in European waters. But our Air Force on which so much depends, so far from overtaking Germany, is actually falling farther and farther behind. If we are to place ourselves in security we must throw ourselves into the business of national defence with the vigour and concentration which Germany now displays.

It is no small or local cause we plead tonight. We must march in the good company of nations and we march under the standards of Law, of Justice and of Freedom. We must gather together around the joint strength of Britain and France and under the authority of the League all countries prepared to resist, and if possible to prevent acts of violent aggression. There is the path to safety. There are the only guarantees of Freedom. There, on the rock of the Covenant of the League of Nations alone, can we build high and enduring the temple and towers of Peace.

Free Trade Hall, Manchester, May 9, 1938

I have a tendency against which I should, perhaps, be on my guard, to swim against the stream.

At all times, according to my lights and throughout the changing scenes through which we are all hurried, I have always faithfully served two public causes which, I think, stand supreme—the maintenance of the enduring greatness of Britain and her Empire, and the historical continuity of our island life.

A state of society where men may not speak their minds, where children denounce their parents to the police, where a business man or small shopkeeper ruins his competitor by telling tales about his private opinions: such a state of society cannot long endure if brought into contact with the healthy outside world. The light of civilized progress with its tolerances and co-operation, with its dignities and joys, has often in the past been blotted out. But I hold the belief that we have now at last got far enough ahead of barbarism to control it, and to avert it, if only we realize what is afoot and make up our minds in time. We shall do it in the end.

Broadcast to America, October 16, 1938

All the years that I have been in the House of Commons I have always said to myself one thing: 'Do not interrupt,' and I have never been able to keep to that resolution.

The Times is speechless, and takes three columns to express its speechlessness.

THE MUNICH AGREEMENT 1938

I will begin by saying what everybody would like to ignore or forget but which must nevertheless be stated, namely, that we have sustained a total and unmitigated defeat, and that France has suffered even more than we have. The utmost my right hon. Friend the Prime Minister has been able to secure by all his immense exertions, by all the great efforts and mobilization which took place in this country, and by all the anguish and strain through which we have passed in this country, the utmost he has been able to gain for Czechoslovakia in the matters which were in dispute has been that the German dictator, instead of snatching the victuals from the table, has been content to have them served to him course by course.

The Chancellor of the Exchequer [Sir John Simon] said it was the first time Herr Hitler had been made to retract—I think that was the word—in any degree. We really must not waste time after all this long Debate upon the difference between the positions reached at Berchtesgaden, at Godesberg and at Munich. They can be very simply epitomized, if the House will permit me to vary the metaphor. £1 was demanded at the pistol's point. When it was given, £2 were demanded at the pistol's point. Finally, the dictator consented to take £1 17s. 6d. and the rest in promises of good will for the future.

Now I come to the point, which was mentioned to me just now from some quarters of the House, about the saving of peace. No one has been a more resolute and uncompromising struggler for peace than the Prime Minister. Everyone knows that. Never has there been such intense and undaunted determination to maintain and secure peace. That is quite true. Nevertheless, I am not quite clear why there was so much danger of Great Britain or France being involved in a war with Germany at this juncture if, in fact, they were ready all along to sacrifice Czechoslovakia. The terms which the Prime Minister brought back with him could easily have been agreed, I believe, through the ordinary diplomatic channels at any time during the summer. And I will say this, that I believe the Czechs, left to themselves and told they were going to get no help from the Western Powers, would have been able to make better terms than they have got after all this tremendous perturbation; they could hardly have had worse.

There never can be any absolute certainty that there will be a fight if one side is determined that it will give way completely. When one reads the Munich terms, when one sees what is happening in Czechoslovakia from hour to hour, when one is sure, I will not say of Parliamentary approval but of Parliamentary acquiescence, when the Chancellor of the Exchequer makes a speech which at any rate tries to put it in a very powerful and persuasive manner the fact that, after all, it was inevitable and indeed righteous : when we saw all this—and everyone on this side of the House, including many members of the Conservative Party who are vigilant and careful guardians of the national interest, is quite clear that nothing vitally affecting us was at stake—it seems to me that one must ask : What was all the trouble and fuss about?

The resolve was taken by the British and the French Governments. Let me say that it is very important to realize that it is by no means a question which the British Government only have had to decide. I very much admire the manner in which, in the House, all references of a recriminatory nature have been repressed. But it must be realized that this resolve did not emanate particularly from one or other of the Governments but was a resolve for which both must share in common the responsibility. When this resolve was taken and the course was followed—you may say it was wise or unwise, prudent or short-sighted—once it had been decided not to make the defence of Czechoslovakia a matter of war, then there was really no reason, if the matter had been handled during the summer in the ordinary way, to call into being all this formidable apparatus of crisis. I think that point should be considered.

We are asked to vote for this Motion[1] which has been put upon the Paper, and it is certainly a Motion couched in very uncontroversial terms, as, indeed, is the Amendment moved from the Opposition side. I have always held the view that the maintenance of peace depends upon the accumulation of deterrents against the aggressor, coupled with a sincere effort to redress grievances. Herr Hitler's victory, like so many of the famous struggles that have governed the fate of the world, was won upon the narrowest of margins. After the seizure of Austria in March we faced this problem in our Debates. I ventured to appeal to the Government to go a little farther than the Prime Minister went, and to give a pledge that in conjunction with France and other Powers they would guarantee the security of Czechoslovakia while the Sudeten-Deutsch question was being examined

[1] 'That this House approves the policy of His Majesty's Government by which war was averted in the recent crisis and supports their efforts to secure a lasting peace.'

either by a League of Nations Commission or some other impartial body, and I still believe that if that course had been followed events would not have fallen into this disastrous state. I agree very much with my right hon. Friend the Member for Sparkbrook [Mr. Amery] when he said on that occasion: 'Do one thing or the other; either say you will disinterest yourself in the matter altogether or take the step of giving a guarantee which will have the greatest chance of securing protection for that country.'

France and Great Britain together, especially if they had maintained a close contact with Russia, which certainly was not done, would have been able in those days in the summer, when they had the prestige, to influence many of the smaller States of Europe; and I believe they could have determined the attitude of Poland. Such a combination, prepared at a time when the German dictator was not deeply and irrevocably committed to his new adventure, would, I believe, have given strength to all those forces in Germany which resisted this departure, this new design. They were varying forces—those of a military character which declared that Germany was not ready to undertake a world war, and all that mass of moderate opinion and popular opinion which dreaded war, and some elements of which still have some influence upon the Government. Such action would have given strength to all that intense desire for peace which the helpless German masses share with their British and French fellow men, and which, as we have been reminded, found a passionate and rarely permitted vent in the joyous manifestations with which the Prime Minister was acclaimed in Munich.

All these forces, added to the other deterrents which combinations of Powers, great and small, ready to stand firm upon the front of law and for the ordered remedy of grievances, would have formed, might well have been effective. Between submission and immediate war there was this third alternative, which gave a hope not only of peace but of justice. It is quite true that such a policy in order to succeed demanded that Britain should declare straight out and a long time beforehand that she would, with others, join to defend Czechoslovakia against an unprovoked aggression. His Majesty's Government refused to give that guarantee when it would have saved the situation, yet in the end they gave it when it was too late, and now, for the future, they renew it when they have not the slightest power to make it good.

All is over. Silent, mournful, abandoned, broken, Czechoslovakia recedes into the darkness. She has suffered in every respect by her association with the Western democracies and with the League of Nations, of which she has always been an obedient servant. She has suffered in particular from her association with France, under whose guidance and policy she has been actuated for so long. The very measure taken by His Majesty's Government in the Anglo-French Agreement to give her the best chance possible, namely, the 50 per cent clean-cut in certain districts instead of a plebiscite, have turned to her detriment, because there is to be a plebiscite too in wide areas, and those other Powers who had claims have also come down upon the helpless victim. Those municipal elections upon whose voting the basis is taken for the 50 per cent cut were held on issues which had nothing to do with joining Germany. When I saw Herr Henlein over here he assured me that was not the desire of his people. Positive statements were made that it was only a question of home rule, of having a position of their own in the Czechoslovakian State. No one has a right to say that the plebiscite which is to be taken in areas under Saar conditions, and the clean-cut of the 50 per cent areas—that those two operations together amount in the slightest degree to a verdict of self-determination. It is a fraud and a farce to invoke that name.

We in this country, as in other Liberal and democratic countries, have a perfect right to exalt the principle of self-determination, but it comes ill out of the mouths of those in totalitarian States who deny even the smallest element of toleration to every section and creed within their bounds. But, however you put it, this particular block of land, this mass of human beings to be handed over, has never expressed the desire to go into the Nazi rule. I do not believe that even now, if their opinion could be asked, they would exercise such an opinion.

What is the remaining position of Czechoslovakia? Not only are they politically mutilated, but, economically and financially, they are in complete confusion. Their banking, their railway arrangements, are severed and broken, their industries are curtailed, and the movement of their population is most cruel. The Sudeten miners, who are all Czechs and whose families have lived in that area for centuries, must now flee into an area where there are hardly any mines left for them to work. It is a tragedy which has occurred. There must always be the most profound regret and a sense of vexation in British hearts at the treatment and misfortunes which have overcome the Czechoslovakian Republic. They have not ended here. At any moment there may be a hitch in the programme. At any moment there may be an order for Herr Goebbels to start again his propaganda of calumny and lies; at any moment an incident may be provoked, and now that the fortress line is turned what is there to stop the will of the conqueror? Obviously, we are not in a position to give them the slightest help at the present time, except what everyone is glad to know has been done, the financial aid which the Government have

Churchill as a Harrow schoolboy in 1889.

Earl Lloyd George as War Prime Minister and
Mr. Churchill as First Lord of the Admiralty in
Whitehall, October 1915.

Churchill with the Kaiser at German Army manoeuvres, 1909.

Winston Churchill, June 1943.

promptly produced.

I venture to think that in future the Czechoslovak State cannot be maintained as an independent entity. I think you will find that in a period of time which may be measured by years, but may be measured only by months, Czechoslovakia will be engulfed in the Nazi regime. Perhaps they may join it in despair or in revenge. At any rate, that story is over and told. But we cannot consider the abandonment and ruin of Czechoslovakia in the light only of what happened only last month. It is the most grievous consequence of what we have done and of what we have left undone in the last five years— five years of futile good intentions, five years of eager search for the line of least resistance, five years of uninterrupted retreat of British power, five years of neglect of our air defences. Those are the features which I stand here to expose and which marked an improvident stewardship for which Great Britain and France have dearly to pay. We have been reduced in those five years from a position of security so overwhelming and so unchallengeable that we never cared to think about it. We have been reduced from a position where the very word 'war' was considered one which could be used only by persons qualifying for a lunatic asylum. We have been reduced from a position of safety and power— power to do good, power to be generous to a beaten foe, power to make terms with Germany, power to give her proper redress for her grievances, power to stop her arming if we chose, power to take any step in strength or mercy or justice which we thought right—reduced in five years from a position safe and unchallenged to where we stand now.

When I think of the fair hopes of a long peace which still lay before Europe at the beginning of 1933 when Herr Hitler first obtained power, and of all the oppor-

129

tunities of arresting the growth of the Nazi power which have been thrown away, when I think of the immense combinations and resources which have been neglected or squandered, I cannot believe that a parallel exists in the whole course of history. So far as this country is concerned the responsibility must rest with those who have had the undisputed control of our political affairs. They neither prevented Germany from rearming, nor did they rearm ourselves in time. They quarrelled with Italy without saving Ethiopia. They exploited and discredited the vast institution of the League of Nations and they neglected to make alliances and combinations which might have repaired previous errors, and thus they left us in the hour of trial without adequate national defence or effective international security.

In my holiday I thought it was a chance to study the reign of King Ethelred the Unready. The House will remember that that was a period of great misfortune, in which, from the strong position which we had gained during the descendants of King Alfred, we fell very swiftly into chaos. It was the period of Danegeld and of foreign pressure. I must say that the rugged words of the *Anglo-Saxon Chronicle*, written a thousand years ago, seemed to me apposite, at least as apposite as those quotations from Shakespeare with which we have been regaled by the last speaker from the Opposition Bench. Here is what the *Anglo-Saxon Chronicle* said, and I think the words apply very much to our treatment of Germany and our relations with her. 'All these calamities fell upon us because of evil counsel, because tribute was not offered to them at the right time nor yet were they resisted; but when they had done the most evil, then was peace made with them.' That is the wisdom of the past, for all wisdom is not new wisdom.

I have ventured to express those views in justifying

myself for not being able to support the Motion which is moved tonight, but I recognize that this great matter of Czechoslovakia, and of British and French duty there, has passed into history. New developments may come along, but we are not here to decide whether any of those steps should be taken or not. They have been taken. They have been taken by those who had a right to take them because they bore the highest executive responsibility under the Crown. Whatever we may think of it, we must regard those steps as belonging to the category of affairs which are settled beyond recall. The past is no more, and one can only draw comfort if one feels that one has done one's best to advise rightly and wisely and in good time. I, therefore, turn to the future, and to our situation as it is today. Here, again, I am sure I shall have to say something which will not be at all welcome.

We are in the presence of a disaster of the first magnitude which has befallen Great Britain and France. Do not let us blind ourselves to that. It must now be accepted that all the countries of Central and Eastern Europe will make the best terms they can with the triumphant Nazi power. The system of alliances in Central Europe upon which France has relied for her safety has been swept away, and I can see no means by which it can be reconstituted. The road down the Danube Valley to the Black Sea, the road which leads as far as Turkey, has been opened. In fact, if not in form, it seems to me that all those countries of Middle Europe, all those Danubian countries, will, one after another, be drawn into this vast system of power politics—not only power military politics, but power economic politics—radiating from Berlin, and I believe this can be achieved quite smoothly and swiftly and will not necessarily entail the firing of a single shot.

But what will be the position, I want to know, of France and England this year and the year afterwards? What will be the position of that Western front of which we are in full authority the guarantors? The German army at the present time is more numerous than that of France, though not nearly so matured or perfected. Next year it will grow much larger, and its maturity will be more complete. Relieved from all the anxiety in the East, and having secured resources which will greatly if not entirely remove, the deterrent of a naval blockade, the rulers of Nazi Germany will have a free choice open to them as to what direction they will turn their eyes. If the Nazi dictator should choose to look westward, as he may, bitterly will France and England regret the loss of that fine army of ancient Bohemia which was estimated last week to require not fewer than 30 German divisions for its destruction.

Can we blind ourselves to the great change which has taken place in the military situation, and to the dangers we have to meet? We are in process, I believe, of adding in four years, four battalions to the British army. No fewer than two have already been completed. Here are at least thirty divisions which must now be taken into consideration upon the French front, besides the twelve that were captured when Austria was engulfed. Many people, no doubt, honestly believe that they are only giving away the interests of Czechoslovakia, whereas I fear we shall find that we have deeply compromised, and perhaps fatally endangered, the safety and even the independence of Great Britain and France. This is not merely a question of giving up the German colonies, as I am sure we shall be asked to do. Nor is it a question only of losing influence in Europe. It goes far deeper than that. You have to consider the character of the Nazi movement and the rule which it implies. The Prime

Minister desires to see cordial relations between this country and Germany. There is no difficulty at all in having cordial relations between the peoples. Our hearts go out to them. But they have no power. But never will you have friendship with the present German Government. You must have diplomatic and correct relations, but there can never be friendship between the British democracy and the Nazi power, that power which spurns Christian ethics, which cheers its onward course by a barbarous paganism, which vaunts the spirit of aggression and conquest, which derives strength and perverted pleasure from persecution, and uses, as we have seen, with pitiless brutality the threat of murderous force. That power cannot ever be the trusted friend of the British democracy.

What I find unendurable is the sense of our country falling into the power, into the orbit and influence of Nazi Germany, and of our existence becoming dependent upon their good will or pleasure. It is to prevent that that I have tried my best to urge the maintenance of every bulwark of defence—first, the timely creation of an Air Force superior to anything within striking distance of our shores; secondly, the gathering together of the collective strength of many nations; and thirdly, the making of alliances and military conventions, all within the Covenant, in order to gather together forces at any rate to restrain the onward movement of this power. It has all been in vain. Every position has been successively undermined and abandoned on specious and plausible excuses.

We do not want to be led upon the high road to becoming a satellite of the German Nazi system of European domination. In a very few years, perhaps in a very few months, we shall be confronted with demands with which we shall no doubt be invited to comply.

Those demands may effect the surrender of territory or the surrender of liberty. I foresee and foretell that the policy of submission will carry with it restrictions upon the freedom of speech and debate in Parliament, on public platforms, and discussions in the Press, for it will be said—indeed, I hear it said sometimes now—that we cannot allow the Nazi system of dictatorship to be criticized by ordinary common English politicians. Then, with a Press under control, in part direct but more potently indirect, with every organ of public opinion doped and chloroformed into acquiescence, we shall be conducted along further stages of our journey.

I have been casting about to see how measures can be taken to protect us from this advance of the Nazi power, and to secure those forms of life which are so dear to us. What is the sole method that is open? The sole method that is open is for us to regain our old island independence by acquiring that supremacy in the air which we were promised, the security in our air defences which we were assured we had, and thus to make ourselves an island once again. That, in all this grim outlook, shines out as the overwhelming fact. An effort at rearmament the like of which has not been seen ought to be made forthwith, and all the resources of this country and all its united strength should be bent to that task. I was very glad to see that Lord Baldwin yesterday in the House of Lords said that he would mobilize industry tomorrow. But I think it would have been much better if Lord Baldwin had said that two and a half years ago, when everyone demanded a Ministry of Supply. I will venture to say to hon. Gentlemen sitting here behind the Government Bench, hon. Friends of mine, whom I thank for the patience with which they have listened to what I have to say, that they have some responsibility for all this, too, because, if they had given one tithe of the cheers they have lavished upon this transaction of Czechoslovakia to the small band of Members who were endeavouring to get timely rearmament set in motion, we should not now be in the position in which we are. Hon. Gentlemen opposite, and hon. Members on the Liberal benches, are not entitled to throw these stones. I remember for two years having to face, not only the Government's deprecation, but their stern disapproval. Lord Baldwin has now given the signal, tardy though it may be; let us at least obey it.

After all, there are no secrets now about what happened in the air and in the mobilization of our anti-aircraft defences. These matters have been, as my hon. and gallant Friend the Member for the Abbey Division said, seen by thousands of people. They can form their own opinions of the character of the statements which have been persistently made to us by Ministers on this subject. Who pretends now that there is air parity with Germany? Who pretends now that our anti-aircraft defences were adequately manned or armed? We know that the German General Staff are well informed upon these subjects, but the House of Commons has hitherto not taken seriously its duty of requiring to assure itself on these matters. The Home Secretary[1] said the other night that he would wecome investigation. Many things have been done which reflect the greatest credit upon the administration. But the vital matters are what we want to know about. I have asked again and again during these three years for a secret Session where these matters could be thrashed out, or for an investigation by a Select Committee of the House, or for some other method. I ask now that, when we meet again in the autumn, that should be a matter on which the Government should take the House into its confidence, because

[1] Sir Samuel Hoare, now Lord Templewood.

we have a right to know where we stand and what measures are being taken to secure our position.

I do not grudge our loyal, brave people, who were ready to do their duty no matter what the cost, who never flinched under the strain of last week—I do not grudge them the natural, spontaneous outburst of joy and relief when they learned that the hard ordeal would no longer be required of them at the moment; but they should know the truth. They should know that there has been gross neglect and deficiency in our defences; they should know that we have sustained a defeat without a war, the consequences of which will travel far with us along our road; they should know that we have passed an awful milestone in our history, when the whole equilibrium of Europe has been deranged, and that the terrible words have for the time being been pronounced against the Western democracies: 'Thou art weighed in the balance and found wanting.' And do not suppose that this is the end. This is only the beginning of the reckoning. This is only the first sip, the first foretaste of a bitter cup which will be proffered to us year by year unless by a supreme recovery of moral health and martial vigour, we arise again and take our stand for freedom as in the olden time.

House of Commons, October 5, 1938

Writing a long and substantial book is like having a friend and companion at your side, to whom you can always turn for comfort and amusement, and whose society becomes more attractive as a new and widening field of interest is lighted in the mind.

In the art of drafting [Income Tax Law] there seems to be a complete disdain of the full stop, and even the humble colon is an object to be avoided.

We must not turn from the path of duty. If the British Empire is fated to pass from life into history, we must hope it will not be by the slow processes of dispersion and decay, but in some supreme exertion for freedom, for right and for truth. Why is it that from so many lands men look towards us today? It is certainly not because we have gained advantages in a race of armaments, or have scored a point by some deeply-planned diplomatic intrigue, or because we exhibit the blatancy and terrorism of ruthless power. It is because we stand on the side of the general need. In the British Empire we not only look out across the seas towards each other, but backwards to our own history, to Magna Charta, to Habeas Corpus, to the Petition of Right, to Trial by Jury, to the English Common Law and to Parliamentary Democracy. These are the milestones and monuments that mark the path along which the British race has marched to leadership and freedom. And over all this, uniting each Dominion with the other and uniting us all with our majestic past, is the golden circle of the Crown. What is within the circle? Not only the glory of an ancient unconquered people, but the hope, the sure hope of a broadening life for hundreds of millions of men.

Canada Club, April 20, 1939

In this solemn hour it is a consolation to recall and to dwell upon our repeated efforts for peace. All have been ill-starred, but all have been faithful and sincere. This is of the highest moral value—and not only moral value, but practical value—at the present time, because the wholehearted concurrence of scores of millions of men and women, whose co-operation is indispensable and whose comradeship and brotherhood are indispensable, is the only foundation upon which the trial and tribulation of modern war can be endured and surmounted. This moral conviction alone affords that everfresh resilience which renews the strength and energy of people in long, doubtful and dark days. Outside, the storms of war may blow and the lands may be lashed with the fury of its gales, but in our own hearts this Sunday morning there is peace. Our hands may be active, but our consciences are at rest.

We must not underrate the gravity of the task which lies before us or the tenerity of the ordeal, to which we shall not be found unequal. We must expect many disappointments, and many unpleasant surprises, but we may be sure that the task which we have freely accepted is one not beyond the compass and the strength of the British Empire and the French Republic. The Prime Minister said it was a sad day, and that is indeed true, but at the present time there is another note which may be present, and that is a feeling of thankfulness that, if these great trials were to come upon our island, there is a generation of Britons here now ready to prove itself not unworthy of the days of yore and not unworthy of those great men, the fathers of our land, who laid the foundations of our laws and shaped the greatness of our country.

This is not a question of fighting for Danzig or fighting for Poland. We are fighting to save the whole world from the pestilence of Nazi tyranny and in defence of all that is most sacred to man. This is no war of domination or imperial aggrandisement or material gain; no war to shut any country out of its sunlight and means of progress. It is a war, viewed in its inherent quality, to establish, on impregnable rocks, the rights of the individual, and it is a war to establish and revive the stature of man. Perhaps it might seem a paradox that a war undertaken in the name of liberty and right should require, as a necessary part of its processes, the surrender for the time being of so many of the dearly valued liberties and rights. In these last few days the House of Commons has been voting dozens of Bills which hand over to the executive our most dearly valued traditional liberties. We are sure that these liberties will be in hands which will not abuse them, which will use them for no class or party interests, which will cherish and guard them, and we look forward to the day, surely and confidently we look forward to the day, when our liberties and rights will be retired to us, and when we shall be able to share them with the peoples to whom such blessings are unknown.

The House of Commons, September 3, 1939

We must not allow our insular pride to blind us to the fact that some of these foreigners are quite intelligent, that they have an extraordinary knack on occasion of rising fully up to the level of British comprehension.

It is always wise to look ahead, but difficult to look further than you can see.

The spirit of all our forces serving on salt water has never been more strong and high than now. The warrior heroes of the past may look down, as Nelson's monument looks down upon us now, without any feeling that the island race has lost its daring or that the examples they set in bygone centuries have faded as the generations have succeeded one another. It was not for nothing that Admiral Harwood, as he instantly at full speed attacked an enemy which might have sunk any one of his ships by a single successful salvo from its far heavier guns, flew Nelson's immortal signal of which neither the new occasion, nor the conduct of all ranks and ratings, nor the final result were found unworthy.

To the glorious tale of the action off the Plate, there has recently been added an epilogue—the rescue last week by the *Cossack* and her flotilla, under the nose of the enemy and amid the tangles of one-sided neutrality, of the British captives taken from the sunken German raider. Their rescue at the very moment when these unhappy men were about to be delivered over to German bondage, proves that the long arm of British sea power can be stretched out, not only for foes but also for faithful friends. And to Nelson's signal of 135 years ago, 'England expects that every man will do his duty', there may now be added last week's not less proud reply : 'The Navy is here !'

Guildhall, February 23, 1940

Come then : let us to the task, to the battle, to the toil—each to our part, each to our station. Fill the armies, rule the air, pour out the munitions, strangle the U-boats, sweep the mines, plough the land, build the ships, guard the streets, succour the wounded, uplift the downcast, and honour the brave. Let us go forward together in all parts of the Empire, in all parts of the island. There is not a week, nor a day, nor an hour to lose.

Free Trade Hall, January 27, 1940

In our country public men are proud to be the servants of the people. They would be ashamed to be their masters. Ministers of the Crown feel themselves strengthened by having at their side the House of Commons and the House of Lords sitting with great regularity, and acting as a continual stimulus to their activities. Of course it is quite true that there is often severe criticism of the Government in both Houses. We do not resent the well-meant criticism of any man who wishes to win the war. We do not shrink from fair criticism, and that is the most dangerous of all. On the countrary, we take it earnestly to heart and seek to profit by it. Criticism in the body politic is like pain in the human body. It is not pleasant, but where would the body be without it? No health or sensibility would be possible without continued correctives and warnings of pain.

Free Trade Hall, Manchester, January 27, 1940

On Friday evening last I received His Majesty's commission to form a new administration. It was the evident wish and will of Parliament and the nation that this should be conceived on the broadest possible basis and that it should include all parties, both those who supported the late Government and also the parties of the Opposition. I have completed the most important part of this task. A War Cabinet has been formed of five Members, representing, with the Opposition Liberals, the unity of the nation. The three party leaders have agreed to serve, either in the War Cabinet or in high executive office. The three fighting services have been filled. It was necessary that this should be done in one single day, on account of the extreme urgency and rigour of events. A number of other key positions were filled yesterday, and I am submitting a further list to His Majesty tonight. I hope to complete the appointment of the principal Ministers during tomorrow. The appointment of the other Ministers usually takes a little longer, but I trust that, when Parliament meets again, this part of my task will be completed, and that the administration will be complete in all respects.

I considered it in the public interest to suggest that the House should be summoned to meet today. Mr. Speaker agreed, and took the necessary steps, in accordance with the powers conferred upon him by the Resolution of the House. At the end of the proceedings today, the adjournment of the House will be proposed until Tuesday, May 21, with, of course, provision for earlier meeting if need be. The business to be considered during that week will be notified to Members at the earliest opportunity. I now invite the House, by the Resolution which stands in my name, to record its approval of the steps taken and to declare its confidence in the new Government.

To form an administration of this scale and complexity is a serious undertaking in itself, but it must be remembered that we are in the preliminary stage of one of the greatest battles in history, that we are in action at many points in Norway and in Holland, that we have to be prepared in the Mediterranean, that the air battle is continuous and that many preparations have to be made here at home. In this crisis I hope I may be pardoned if I do not address the House at any length today. I hope that any of my friends and colleagues, or former colleagues, who are affected by the political reconstruction, will make all allowance for any lack of ceremony with which it has been necessary to act. I would say to the House, as I said to those who have joined this Government: 'I have nothing to offer but blood, toil, tears and sweat.'

We have before us an ordeal of the most grievous kind. We have before us many, many long months of struggle and of suffering. You ask what is our policy? I will say: It is to wage war, by sea, land and air, with all our might and with all the strength that God can give us: to wage war against a monstrous tyranny, never surpassed in the dark, lamentable catalogue of human crime. That is our policy. You ask, What is our aim? I can answer in one word: Victory—victory at all costs, victory in spite of all terror, victory, however long and hard the road may be; for without victory, there is no survival. Let that be realized; no survival for the British Empire; no survival for all that the British Empire has stood for, no survival for the urge and impulse of the ages, that mankind will move forward towards its goal. But I take up my task with buoyancy and hope. I feel sure that our cause will not be suffered to fail among men. At this time I feel entitled to claim the aid of all, and I say, 'Come, then, let us go forward together with our united strength.'

A speech to the House of Commons, May 13, 1940

Having received His Majesty's commission, I have formed an administration of men and women of every party and of almost every point of view. We have differed and quarrelled in the past; but now one bond unites us all—to wage war until victory is won, and never to surrender ourselves to servitude and shame, whatever the cost and the agony may be. This is one of the most awe-striking periods in the long history of France and Britain. It is also beyond doubt the most sublime. Side by side, unaided except by their kith and kin in the great Dominions and by the wide Empires which rest beneath their shield—side by side, the British and French peoples have advanced to rescue not only Europe but mankind from the foulest and most soul-destroying tyranny which has ever darkened and stained the pages of history. Behind them—behind us—behind the armies and fleets of Britain and France—gather a group of shattered States and bludgeoned races: the Czechs, the Poles, the Norwegians, the Danes, the Dutch, the Belgians—upon all of whom the long night of barbarism will descend, unbroken even by a star of hope, unless we conquer, as conquer we must; as conquer we shall.

Today is Trinity Sunday. Centuries ago words were written to be a call and a spur to the faithful servants of truth and justice : 'Arm yourselves and be ye men of valour, and be in readiness for the conflict; for it is better for us to perish in battle than to look upon the outrage of our nation and our altar. As the Will of God is in Heaven, even so let it be.'

Broadcast, May 19, 1940

From the moment that the French defences at Sedan and on the Meuse were broken at the end of the second week of May, only a rapid retreat to Amiens and the south could have saved the British and French armies who had entered Belgium at the appeal of the Belgian King; but this strategic fact was not immediately realized. The French High Command hoped they would be able to close the gap, and the armies of the north were under their orders. Moreover, a retirement of this kind would have involved almost certainly the destruction of the fine Belgian Army of over twenty divisions and the abandonment of the whole of Belgium. Therefore, when the force and scope of the German penetration were realized and when a new French generalissimo, General Weygand, assumed command in place of General Gamelin, an effort was made by the French and British armies in Belgium to keep on holding the right hand of the Belgians and to give their own right hand to a newly created French army which was to have advanced across the Somme in great strength to grasp it.

However, the German eruption swept like a sharp scythe around the right and rear of the armies of the north. Eight or nine armoured divisions, each of about four hundred armoured vehicles of different kinds, but carefully assorted to be complementary and divisible into small self-contained units, cut off all communications between us and the main French armies. It severed our own communications for food and ammunition, which ran first to Amiens and afterwards through Abbeville, and it shore its way up the coast to Boulogne and Calais, and almost to Dunkirk. Behind this armoured and mechanized onslaught came a number of German divisions in lorries, and behind them again there plodded comparatively slowly the dull brute mass of the ordinary German Army and German people, always so ready to be led to the trampling down in other lands of liberties and comforts which they have never known in their own.

I have said this armoured scythe-stroke almost reached Dunkirk—almost but not quite. Boulogne and Calais were the scenes of desperate fighting. The Guards defended Boulogne for a while and were then withdrawn by orders from this country. The Rifle Brigade, the 60th Rifles, and the Queen Victoria's Rifles, with a battalion of British tanks and 1,000 Frenchmen, in all about 4,000 strong, defended Calais to the last. The British brigadier was given an hour to surrender. He spurned the offer, and four days of intense street fighting passed before silence reigned over Calais, which marked the end of a memorable resistance. Only thirty unwounded survivors were brought off by the Navy and we do not know the fate of their comrades. Their sacrifice, however, was not in vain. At least two armoured divisions, which otherwise would have been turned against the British Expeditionary Force, had to be sent to overcome them. They have added another page to the glories of the light divisions, and the time gained enabled the Graveline waterlines to be flooded and to be held by the French troops.

Thus it was that the port of Dunkirk was kept open. When it was found impossible for the armies of the north to reopen their communications to Amiens with the main French armies, only one choice remained. It seemed, indeed, forlorn. The Belgian, British and French armies were almost surrounded. Their sole line of retreat was to a single port and to its neighbouring beaches. They were passed on every side by heavy attacks and far out-numbered in the air.

When a week ago today I asked the House to fix this afternoon as the occasion for a statement, I feared it would be my hard lot to announce the greatest military disaster in our long history. I thought—and some good judges agreed with me—that perhaps 20,000 or 30,000 men might be re-embarked. But it certainly seemed that the whole of the French First Army and the whole of the British Expeditionary Force north of the Amiens–Abbeville gap, would be broken up in the open field or else would have to capitulate for lack of food and ammunition. These were the hard and heavy tidings for which I called upon the House and the nation to prepare themselves a week ago. The whole root and core and brain of the British Army, on which and around which we were to build, and are to build, the great British armies in the later years of the war, seemed about to perish upon the field or to be led into an ignominious and starving captivity.

That was the prospect a week ago. But another blow which might well have proved final was yet to fall upon us. The King of the Belgians had called upon us to come to his aid. Had not this ruler and his Government severed themselves from the Allies, who rescued their country from extinction in the late war, and had they not sought refuge in what has proved to be a fatal neutrality, the French and British Armies might well at the outset have saved not only Belgium but perhaps even Poland. Yet at the last moment when Belgium was already invaded, King Leopold called upon us to come to his aid, and even at the last moment we came. He and his brave, efficient army, nearly half a million strong, guarded our left flank and thus kept open our only line of retreat to the sea. Suddenly, without prior consultation, with the least possible notice, without the advice of his Ministers and upon his own personal act, he sent a plenipotentiary to the German Command, surrendered his army and exposed our whole flank and means of retreat.

I asked the House a week ago to suspend its judgment because the facts were not clear, but I do not feel that any reason now exists why we should not form our own opinions upon this pitiful episode. The surrender of the Belgian Army compelled the British at the shortest notice to cover a flank to the sea more than thirty miles in length. Otherwise all would have been cut off, and all would have shared the fate to which King Leopold had condemned the finest army his country had ever formed. So in doing this and in exposing this flank, as anyone who followed the operations on the map will see, contact was lost between the British and two out of the three corps forming the First French Army, who were still farther from the coast than we were, and it seemed impossible that any large number of Allied troops could reach the coast.

The enemy attacked on all sides with great strength and fierceness, and their main power, the power of their far more numerous air force, was thrown into the battle or else concentrated upon Dunkirk and the beaches. Pressing in upon the narrow exit, both from the east and from the west, the enemy began to fire with cannon upon the beaches by which alone the shipping could approach or depart. They sowed magnetic mines in the channels and seas; they sent repeated waves of hostile aircraft, sometimes more than a hundred strong in one formation, to cast their bombs upon the single pier that remained, and upon the sand dunes upon which the troops had their eyes for shelter. Their U-boats, one of which was sunk, and their motor launches took their toll of the vast traffic which now began. For four or five days an intense struggle reigned. All their armoured divisions—or what was left of them —together with great masses of infantry and artillery, hurled themselves in vain upon the ever-narrowing, ever-contracting appendix within which the British and French armies fought.

Meanwhile, the Royal Navy, with the willing help of countless merchant seamen, strained every nerve to embark the British and Allied troops; 220 light warships and 560 other vessels were engaged. They had to operate upon the difficult coast, often in adverse weather, under an almost ceaseless hail of bombs and an increasing concentration of artillery fire. Nor were the seas, as I have said, themselves free from mines and torpedoes. It was in conditions such as these that our men carried on, with little or no rest, for days and nights on end, making trip after trip across the dangerous waters, bringing with them always men whom they had rescued. The numbers they have brought back are the measure of their devotion and their courage. The hospital ships, which brought off many thousands of British and French wounded, being so plainly marked were a special target for Nazi bombs; but the men and women on board them never faltered in their duty.

Meanwhile, the Royal Air Force, which had already been intervening in the battle, so far as its range would allow, from home bases, now used part of its main metropolitan fighter strength, and struck at the German bombers, and at the fighters which in large numbers protected them. This struggle was protracted and fierce. Suddenly the scene has cleared, the crash and thunder has for the moment—but only for the moment—died away. A miracle of deliverance, achieved by valour, by perseverance, by perfect discipline, by faultless service, by resource, by skill, by unconquerable fidelity, is manifest to us all. The enemy was hurled back by the retreating British and French troops. He was so roughly handled that he did not hurry their departure seriously. The Royal Air Force engaged the main strength of the German Air Force, and inflicted upon them losses of at least four to one; and the Navy, using nearly 1,000 ships of all kinds, carried over 335,000 men, French and British, out of the jaws of death and shame, to their native land and to the tasks which lie immediately ahead. We must be very careful not to assign to this deliverance the attributes of a victory. Wars are not won by evacuations. But there was a victory inside this deliverance, which should be noted. It was gained by the Air Force.

When we consider how much greater would be our advantage in defending the air above this island against an overseas attack, I must say that I find in these facts a sure basis upon which practical and reassuring thoughts may rest. I will pay my tribute to these young airmen. The great French Army was very largely, for the time being, cast back and disturbed by the onrush of a few thousands of armoured vehicles. May it not also be that the cause of civilization itself will be defended by the skill and devotion of a few thousand airmen. There never had been, I suppose, in all the world, in all the history of war, such an opportunity for youth. The Knights of the Round Table, the Crusaders, all fall back into the past: not only distant but prosaic; these young men, going forth every morn to guard their native land and all that we stand for, holding in their hands these instruments of colossal and shattering power, of whom it may be said that

'Every morn brought forth a noble chance
And every chance brought forth a noble knight'

deserve our gratitude, as do all the brave men who, in so many ways and on so many occasions, are ready, and continue ready, to give life and all for their native land.

I return to the Army. In the long series of very fierce battles, now on this front, now on that, fighting on three fronts at once, battles fought by two or three divisions against an equal or somewhat larger number of the enemy, and fought fiercely on some of the old grounds that so many of us knew so well, in these battles our losses in men have exceeded 30,000 killed, wounded and missing. I take occasion to express the sympathy of the House to all who have suffered bereavement or who are still anxious. The President of the Board of Trade[1] is not here today. His son has been killed, and many in the House have felt the pangs of affliction in the sharpest form. But I will say this about the missing. We have had a large number of wounded come home safely to this country, but I would say about the missing that there may be very many reported missing who will come back home, some day, in one way or another. In the confusion of this fight it is inevitable that many have been left in positions where honour required no further resistance from them.

Against this loss of over 30,000 men, we can set a far heavier loss certainly inflicted upon the enemy. But

[1] Sir Andrew Duncan.

our losses in material are enormous. We have perhaps lost one-third of the men we lost in the opening days of the battle of March 21, 1918, but we have lost nearly as many guns—nearly 1,000—and all our transport, all the armoured vehicles that were with the Army in the north. This loss will impose a further delay on the expansion of our military strength. That expansion had not been proceeding as fast as we had hoped. The best of all we had to give had gone to the British Expeditionary Force, and although they had not the number of tanks and some articles of equipment which were desirable, they were a very well and finely equipped army. They had the first-fruits of all that our industry had to give, and that is gone. And now here is this further delay. How long it will be, how long it will last, depends upon the exertions which we make in this island. An effort the like of which has never been seen in our records is now being made. Work is proceeding everywhere, night and day, Sundays and weekdays. Capital and labour have cast aside their interests, rights and customs and put them into the common stock. Already the flow of munitions has leapt forward. There is no reason why we should not in a few months overtake the sudden and serious loss that has come upon us, without retarding the development of our general programme.

Nevertheless, our thankfulness at the escape of our Army and so many men, whose loved ones have passed through an agonizing week, must not blind us to the fact that what has happened in France and Belgium is a colossal military disaster. The French Army has been weakened, the Belgian Army has been lost, a large part of those fortified lines upon which so much faith had been reposed is gone, many valuable mining districts and factories have passed into the enemy's possession, the whole of the Channel ports are in his hands, with all the tragic consequences that follow from that, and we must expect another blow to be struck almost immediately at us or at France. We are told that Herr Hitler has a plan for invading the British Isles. This has often been thought of before. When Napoleon lay at Boulogne for a year with his flat-bottomed boats and his Grand Army, he was told by someone, 'There are bitter weeds in England.' There are certainly a great many more of them since the British Expeditionary Force returned.

Turning once again, and this time more generally, to the question of invasion, I would observe that there has never been a period in all these long centuries of which we boast when an absolute guarantee against invasion, still less against serious raids, could have been given to our people. In the days of Napoleon the same wind which would have carried his transports across the Channel might have driven away the blockading fleet. There was always the chance, and it is that chance which has excited and befooled the imaginations of many Continental tyrants. Many are the tales that are told. We are assured that novel methods will be adopted, and when we see the originality of malice, the ingenuity of aggression, which our enemy displays, we may certainly prepare ourselves for every kind of novel stratagem and every kind of brutal and treacherous manoeuvre. I think that no idea is so outlandish that it should not be considered and viewed with a searching, but at the same time, I hope, with a steady eye. We must never forget the solid assurances of sea-power and those which belong to air-power if it can be locally exercised.

I have, myself, full confidence that if all do their duty, if nothing is neglected, and if the best arrangements are made, as they are being made, we shall prove ourselves once again able to defend our island home, to ride out the storm of war, and to outlive the menace of tyranny, if necessary for years, if necessary alone. At any rate, that is what we are going to try to do. That is the resolve of His Majesty's Government—every man of them. That is the will of Parliament and the nation. The British Empire and the French Republic, linked together in their cause and in their need, will defend to the death their native soil, aiding each other like good comrades to the utmost of their strength. Even though large tracts of Europe and many old and famous States have fallen or may fall into the grip of the Gestapo and all the odious apparatus of Nazi rule, we shall not flag or fail. We shall go on to the end, we shall fight in France, we shall fight on the seas and oceans, we shall fight with growing confidence and growing strength in the air, we shall defend our island, whatever the cost may be, we shall fight on the beaches, we shall fight on the landing grounds, we shall fight in the fields and in the streets, we shall fight in the hills; we shall never surrender, and even if, which I do not for a moment believe, this island or a large part of it were subjugated and starving, then our Empire beyond the seas, armed and guarded by the British Fleet, would carry on the struggle, until, in God's good time, the new world, with all its power and might, steps forth to the rescue and liberation of the old.

The House of Commons, June 4, 1940

The news from France is very bad and I grieve for the gallant French people who have fallen into this terrible misfortune. Nothing will alter our feelings towards them or our faith that the genius of France will rise again. What has happened in France makes no difference to our actions and purpose. We have become the sole champions now in arms to defend the world cause. We shall do our best to be worthy of this high honour. We shall defend our island home and with the British Empire we shall fight on unconquerable until the curse of Hitler is lifted from the brows of mankind. We are sure that in the end all will come right.

A broadcast to the people of Britain, June 17, 1940

Never give in! Never give in! Never, Never, Never, Never—in nothing great or small, large or petty—never give in except to convictions of honour and good sense.

We may now ask ourselves: In what way has our position worsened since the beginning of the war? It has worsened by the fact that the Germans have conquered a large part of the coastline of Western Europe, and many small countries have been overrun by them. This aggravates the possibilities of air attack and adds to our naval preoccupations. It in no way diminishes, but on the contrary definitely increases, the power of our long distance blockade. Similarly, the entrance of Italy into the war increases the power of our long-distance blockade. We have stopped the worst leak by that. We do not know whether military resistance will come to an end in France or not, but should it do so, then of course the Germans will be able to concentrate their forces, both military and industrial, upon us. But for the reasons I have given to the House these will not be found so easy to apply. If invasion has become more imminent, as no doubt it has, we, being relieved from the task of maintaining a large army in France, have far larger and more efficient forces to meet it.

If Hitler can bring under his despotic control the industries of the countries he has conquered, this will add greatly to his already vast armament output. On the other hand, this will not happen immediately, and we are now assured of immense, continuous and increasing support in supplies and munitions of all kinds from the United States; and especially of aeroplanes and pilots from the Dominions and across the oceans, coming from regions which are beyond the reach of enemy bombers.

I do not see how any of these factors can operate to our detriment on balance before the winter comes; and the winter will impose a strain upon the Nazi regime, with almost all Europe writhing and starving under its cruel heel, which, for all their ruthlessness, will run them very hard. We must not forget that from the moment when we declared war on September 3 it was always possible for Germany to turn all her Air Force upon this country, together with any other devices of invasion she might conceive, and that France could have done little or nothing to prevent her doing so. We have, therefore, lived under this danger, in principle and in a slightly modified form, during all these months. In the meanwhile, however, we have enormously improved our methods of defence, and we have learned, what we had no right to assume at the beginning, namely, that the individual aircraft and the individual British pilot have a sure and definite superiority. Therefore, in casting up this dread balance-sheet and contemplating our dangers with a disillusioned eye, I see great reason for intense vigilance and exertion, but none whatever for panic or despair.

During the first four years of the last war the Allies experienced nothing but disaster and disappointment. That was our constant fear: one blow after another, terrible losses, frightful dangers. Everything miscarried. And yet at the end of those four years the morale of the Allies was higher than that of the Germans, who had moved from one aggressive triumph to another, and who stood everywhere triumphant invaders of the lands into which they had broken. During that war we repeatedly asked ourselves the question: How are we going to win? And no one was able ever to answer it with much precision, until at the end, quite suddenly, quite unexpectedly, our terrible foe collapsed before us, and we were so glutted with victory that in our folly we threw it away.

We do not yet know what will happen in France or whether the French resistance will be prolonged, both in France and in the French Empire overseas. The French Government will be throwing away great opportunities and casting adrift their future if they do not continue the war in accordance with their treaty obligations, from which we have not felt able to release them. The House will have read the historic declaration in which, at the desire of many Frenchmen—and of our own hearts—we have proclaimed our willingness at the darkest hour in French history to conclude a union of common citizenship in this struggle. However matters may go in France or with the French Government, or other French Governments, we in this island and in the British Empire will never lose our sense of comradeship with the French people. If we are now called upon to endure what they have been suffering, we shall emulate their courage, and if final victory rewards our toils they shall share the gains, aye, and freedom shall be restored to all. We abate nothing of our just demands; not one jot or tittle do we recede. Czechs, Poles, Norwegians, Dutch, Belgians have joined their causes to our own. All these shall be restored.

What General Weygand called the Battle of France is over. I expect that the battle of Britain is about to begin. Upon this battle depends the survival of Christian civilization. Upon it depends our own British life, and the long continuity of our institutions and our Empire. The whole fury and might of the enemy must very soon be turned on us. Hitler knows that he will have to break us in this island or lose the war. If we can stand up to him, all Europe may be free and the life of the world may move forward into broad, sunlit uplands. But if we fail, then the whole world, including the United States, including all that we have known and cared for, will sink into the abyss of a new dark age made more sinister and perhaps more protracted, by the lights of perverted science. Let us therefore brace ourselves to our duties, and so bear ourselves that, if the British Empire and its Commonwealth last for a thousand years, men will still say, 'This was their finest hour.'

House of Commons and broadcast, June 18, 1940

'On what may be the eve of an attempted invasion or battle for our native land, the Prime Minister desires to impress upon all persons holding responsible positions in the Government, in the fighting Services, or in the Civil Departments, their duty to maintain a spirit of alert and confident energy. While every precaution must be taken that time and means afford, there are no grounds for supposing that more German troops can be landed in this country, either from the air or across the sea, than can be destroyed or captured by the strong forces at present under arms. The Royal Air Force is in excellent order and at the highest strength it has yet attained. The German Navy was never so weak, nor the British Army at home so strong as now. The Prime Minister expects all His Majesty's servants in high places to set an example of steadiness and resolution. They should check and rebuke expressions of loose and ill-digested opinion in their circle, or by their subordinates. They should not hesitate to report, or if necessary remove, any officers or officials, who are found to be consciously exercising a disturbing or depressing influence, and whose talk is calculated to spread alarm and despondency. Thus alone they will be worthy of the fighting men, who, in the air, on the sea, and on land, have already met the enemy without any sense of being outmatched in martial qualities.'

Message from Prime Minister, July 4, 1940

And now it has come to us to stand alone in the breach, and face the worst that the tyrant's might and enmity can do. Bearing ourselves humbly before God, but conscious that we serve an unfolding purpose, we are ready to defend our native land against the invasion by which it is threatened. We are fighting by ourselves alone; but we are not fighting for ourselves alone. Here in this strong City of Refuge which enshrines the title-deeds of human progress and is of deep consequence to Christian civilization; here, girt about by the seas and oceans where the Navy reigns; shielded from above by the prowess and devotion of our airmen—we await undismayed the impending assault. Perhaps it will come tonight. Perhaps it will come next week. Perhaps it will never come. We must show ourselves equally capable of meeting a sudden violent shock, or what is perhaps a harder test, a prolonged vigil. But be the ordeal sharp or long, or both, we shall seek no terms, we shall tolerate no parley; we may show mercy—we shall ask for none.

World broadcast, July 14, 1940

The reason why I asked the House to go into Secret Session was not because I had anything particularly secret or momentous to say. It was only because there are some things which it is better for us to talk over among ourselves than when we are overheard by the Germans. I wish to speak about the Sittings of the House and how we are to discharge our Parliamentary duties.

A few days ago I had a notification from the Chiefs of Staff. They considered that the date and time of this meeting of ours today had been so widely advertised that to hold it would be to incur an undue risk, and that it should be put off to some date and hour which had not been publicly announced. I felt, however, that Members would be offended if any course was taken which suggested for a moment that we should shirk our duty out of considerations of personal safety. And then there is all that argument which occurs to everyone of our setting an example, and of the incongruity of our ordering Government Departments, and urging Factory workers to remain at work, while we ourselves did not assemble on particular occasions as we had resolved to do.

House of Commons, Secret Session,
September 17, 1940

These cruel, wanton, indiscriminate bombings of London are, of course, a part of Hitler's invasion plans. He hopes, by killing large numbers of civilians, and women and children, that he will terrorize and cow the people of this mighty imperial city, and make them a burden and an anxiety to the Government and thus distract our attention unduly from the ferocious onslaught he is preparing. Little does he know the spirit of the British nation, or the tough fibre of the Londoners, whose forebears played a leading part in the establishment of Parliamentary institutions and who have been bred to value freedom far above their lives. This wicked man, the repository and embodiment of many forms of soul-destroying hatred, this monstrous product of former wrongs and shame, has now resolved to try to break our famous island race by a process of indiscriminate slaughter and destruction. What he has done is to kindle a fire in British hearts, here and all over the world, which will glow long after all traces of the conflagration he has caused in London have been removed. He has lighted a fire which will burn with a steady and consuming flame until the last vestiges of Nazi tyranny have been burnt out of Europe, and until the Old World—and the New—can join hands to rebuild the temples of man's freedom and man's honour, upon foundations which will not soon or easily be over-thrown.

Broadcast, September 11, 1940

As I see it, we must so arrange that, when any district is smitten by bombs which are flung about at utter random, strong, mobile forces will descend on the scene in power and mercy to conquer the flames, as they have done, to rescue sufferers, provide them with food and shelter, to whisk them away to places of rest and refuge, and to place in their hands leaflets which anyone can understand to reassure them that they have not lost all, because all will share their material loss, and in sharing it, sweep it away. These schemes and measures, pursued on the greatest scale and with fierce energy, will require the concentrated attention of the House in the weeks that lie before us. We have to make a job of this business of living and working under fire, and I have not the slightest doubt that when we have settled down to it, we shall establish conditions which will be a credit to our island society and to the whole British family, and will enable us to maintain the production of those weapons in good time upon which our whole safety and future depend. Thus we shall be able to prove to all our friends and sympathizers in every land, bond or free, that Hitler's act of mass terror against the British nation has failed as conspicuously as his magnetic mine and other attempts to strangle our seaborne trade.

House of Commons, October 8, 1940

My life, such as it has been, has been lived for forty years in the public eye, and very varying opinions are entertained about it—and about particular phases in it. I shall attempt no justification, but this I will venture most humbly to submit and also to declare, because it springs most deeply from the convictions of my heart, that at all times according to my lights and throughout the changing scenes through which we are all hurried I have always faithfully served two public causes which I think stand supreme—the maintenance of the enduring greatness of Britain and her Empire and the historical continuity of our island life.

Alone among the nations of the world we have found the means to combine Empire and liberty. Alone among the peoples we have reconciled democracy and tradition; for long generations, nay, over several centuries, no mortal clash or religious or political gulf has opened in our midst. Alone we have found the way to carry forward the glories of the past through all the storms, domestic and foreign, that have surged about, and thus to bring the labours of our forebears as a splendid inheritance for modern progressive democracy to enjoy.

It is this interplay and interweaving of past and present which in this fearful ordeal has revealed to a wondering world the unconquerable strength of a united nation. It is that which has been the source of our strength. In that achievement, all living parties—Conservative, Liberal, Labour and other parties like the Whigs who have passed away—all have borne a part and all today at the moment of our sorest need share the benefits which have resulted from it.

Caxton Hall, October 9, 1940

Five months have passed since I spoke to the British nation and the Empire on the broadcast. In wartime there is a lot to be said for the motto : 'Deeds, not words.' All the same, it is a good thing to look around from time to time and take stock, and certainly our affairs have prospered in several directions during these last four or five months, far better than most of us would have ventured to hope.

We stood our ground and faced the two dictators in the hour of what seemed their overwhelming triumph, and we have shown ourselves capable, so far, of standing up against them alone. After the heavy defeats of the German Air Force by our fighters in August and September, Herr Hitler did not dare attempt the invasion of this island, although he had every need to do so and although he had made vast preparations. Baffled in this mighty project, he sought to break the spirit of the British nation by the bombing, first of London, and afterwards of our great cities. It has now been proved, to the admiration of the world, and of our friends in the United States, that this form of blackmail by murder and terrorism, so far from weakening the spirit of the British nation, has only roused it to a more intense and universal flame than was ever seen before in any modern community.

The whole British Empire has been proud of the Mother Country, and they long to be with us over here in even larger numbers. We have been deeply conscious of the love for us which has flowed from the Dominions of the Crown across the broad ocean spaces. There is the first of our war aims: to be worthy of that love, and to preserve it.

All through these dark winter months the enemy has had the power to drop three or four tons of bombs upon us for every ton we could send to Germany in return. We are arranging so that presently this will be rather the other way around; but meanwhile, London and our big cities have had to stand their pounding. They remind me of the British squares at Waterloo. They are not squares of soldiers; they do not wear scarlet coats. They are just ordinary English, Scottish and Welsh folk—men, women and children—standing steadfastly together. But their spirit is the same, their glory is the same; and, in the end, their victory will be greater than far-famed Waterloo.

We have broken the back of the winter. The daylight grows. The Royal Air Force grows, and is already certainly master of the daylight air. The attacks may be sharper, but they will be shorter; there will be more opportunities for work and service of all kinds; more opportunities for life. So, if our first victory was the repulse of the invader, our second was the frustration of his acts of terror and torture against our people at home.

Meanwhile, abroad, in October, a wonderful thing happened. One of the two dictators—the crafty, cold-blooded, black-hearted Italian, who had thought to gain an Empire on the cheap by stabbing fallen France in the back, got into trouble. Without the slightest provocation, spurred on by lust of power and brutish greed, Mussolini attacked and invaded Greece, only to be hurled back ignominiously by the heroic Greek Army; who, I will say, with your consent, have revived before our eyes the glories which from the classic age gild their native land. While Signor Mussolini was writhing and smarting under the Greek lash in Albania, Generals Wavell and Wilson, who were charged with the defence of Egypt and of the Suez Canal in accordance with our treaty obligations, whose task seemed at one time so difficult, had recevied very powerful reinforcements of men, cannon, equipment and, above all tanks, which we had sent from our island in spite of the invasion threat. Large numbers of troops from India, Australia and New Zealand had also reached them. Forthwith began that series of victories in Libya which have broken irretrievably the Italian military power on the African Continent. We have all been entertained, and I trust edified, by the exposure and humiliation of another of what Byron called

> Those Pagod things of sabre sway,
> With fronts of brass, and feet of clay.

Here, then, in Libya, is the third considerable event upon which we may dwell with some satisfaction. It is just exactly two months ago, to a day, that I was waiting anxiously, but also eagerly, for the news of the great counter-stroke which had been planned against the Italian invaders of Egypt. The secret had been well kept. The preparations had been well made. But to leap across those seventy miles of desert, and attack an army of ten or eleven divisions, equipped with all the appliances of modern war, who had been fortifying themselves for three months, that was a most hazardous adventure.

When the brilliant decisive victory at Sidi Barrani, with its tens of thousands of prisoners, proved that we had quality, manoeuvring power and weapons superior to the enemy who had boasted so much of his virility and his military virtues, it was evident that all the other

Italian forces in Eastern Libya were in great danger. They could not easily beat a retreat along the coastal road without running the risk of being caught in the open by our armoured divisions and brigades ranging far into the desert in tremendous swoops and scoops. They had to expose themselves to being attacked piecemeal.

General Wavell—nay, all our leaders, and all their lithe, active, ardent men, British, Australian, Indian, in the Imperial Army, saw their opportunity. At that time I ventured to draw General Wavell's attention to the seventh chapter of the Gospel of St. Matthew, at the seventh verse, where, as you all know—or ought to know—it is written : 'Ask and it shall be given; seek, and ye shall find; knock, and it shall be opened unto you.' The Army of the Nile has asked, and it was given; they sought, and they have found; they knocked, and it has been opened unto them. In barely eight weeks, by a campaign which will long be studied as a model of the military art, an advance of over 400 miles has been made. The whole Italian Army in the east of Libya, which was reputed to exceed 150,000 men, has been captured or destroyed. The entire province of Cyrenaica —nearly as big as England and Wales—has been conquered. The unhappy Arab tribes, who have for thirty years suffered from the cruelty of Italian rule, carried in some cases to the point of methodical extermination, these Bedouin survivors have at last seen their oppressors in disorderly flight, or led off in endless droves as prisoners of war.

Egypt and the Suez Canal are safe, and the port, the base and the airfields of Benghazi constitute a strategic point of high consequence to the whole of the war in the Eastern Mediterranean.

This is the time, I think, to speak of the leaders who,

at the head of their brave troops, have rendered this distinguished service to the King. The first and foremost, General Wavell, Commander-in-Chief of all the armies of the Middle East, has proved himself a master of war, sage, painstaking, daring and tireless. But General Wavell has repeatedly asked that others should share his fame.

General Wilson, who actually commands the Army of the Nile, was reputed to be one of our finest tacticians—and few will now deny that quality. General O'Connor commanding the 13th Corps, with General Mackay commanding the splendid Australians, and General Creagh who trained and commanded the various armoured divisions which were employed; these three men executed the complicated and astoundingly rapid movements which were made, and fought the actions which occurred. I have just seen a telegram from General Wavell in which he says that the success at Benghazi was due to the outstanding leadership and resolution of O'Connor and Creagh, ably backed by Wilson.

I must not forget here to point out the amazing mechanical feats of the British tanks, whose design and workmanship have beaten all records and stood up to all trials; and show us how closely and directly the work in the factories at home is linked with the victories abroad.

Of course, none of our plans would have succeeded had not our pilots, under Air Chief Marshal Longmore, wrested the control of the air from a far more numerous enemy. Nor would the campaign itself have been possible if the British Mediterranean Fleet, under Admiral Cunningham, had not chased the Italian Navy into its harbours and sustained every forward surge of the Army with all the flexible resources of sea-power.

How far-reaching these resources are we can see from what happened at dawn this morning, when our Western Mediterranean Fleet, under Admiral Somerville, entered the Gulf of Genoa and bombarded in a shattering manner the naval base from which perhaps a Nazi German expedition might soon have sailed to attack General Weygand in Algeria or Tunis. It is right that the Italian people should be made to feel the sorry plight into which they have been dragged by Dictator Mussolini; and if the cannonade of Genoa, rolling along the coast, reverberating in the mountains, reached the ears of our French comrades in their grief and misery, it might cheer them with the feeling that friends—active friends—are near, and that Britannia rules the waves.

The events in Libya are only part of the story : they are only part of the story of the decline and fall of the Italian Empire, that will not take a future Gibbon so long to write as the original work. Fifteen hundred miles away to the southward a strong British and Indian army, having driven the invaders out of the Sudan, is marching steadily forward through the Italian colony of Eritrea, thus seeking to complete the isolation of all the Italian troops in Abyssinia. Other British forces are entering Abyssinia from the west, while the army gathered in Kenya—in the van of which we may discern the powerful forces of the Union of South Africa, organized by General Smuts—is striking northward along the whole enormous front. Lastly, the Ethiopian patriots, whose independence was stolen five years ago, have risen in arms; and their Emperor, so recently an exile in England, is in their midst to fight for their freedom and his throne. Here, then, we see the beginnings of a process of reparation and of the chastisement of wrongdoing, which reminds us that though the mills of God grind slowly, they grind exceeding small.

While these auspicious events have been carrying us stride by stride from what many people thought a forlorn position, and was certainly a very grave position in May and June, to one which permits us to speak with sober confidence of our power to discharge our duty, heavy though it be, in the future—while this has been happening, a mighty tide of sympathy, of good will and of effective aid, has begun to flow across the Atlantic in support of the world cause which is at stake.

I have been so very careful, since I have been Prime Minister, not to encourage false hopes or prophesy smooth and easy things, and yet the tale that I have to tell today is one which must justly and rightly give us cause for deep thankfulness, and also, I think, for strong comfort and even rejoicing. But now I must dwell upon the more serious, darker and more dangerous aspects of the vast scene of the war. We must all of us have been asking ourselves : what has that wicked man whose crime-stained regime and system are at bay and in the toils—what has he been preparing during these winter months? What new devilry is he planning? What new small country will he overrun or strike down? What fresh form of assault will he make upon our island home and fortress; which—let there be no mistake about it—is all that stands between him and the dominion of the world?

But after all, the fate of this war is going to be settled by what happens on the oceans, in the air and—above all—in this island. It seems now to be certain that the Government and people of the United States intend to supply us with all that is necessary for victory. In the last war the United States sent 2,000,000 men across the Atlantic. But this is not a war of vast armies, firing immense masses of shells at one another. We do not need the gallant armies which are forming throughout the American Union. We do not need them this year, nor next year; nor any year that I can foresee. But we do need most urgently an immense and continuous supply of war materials and technical apparatus of all kinds. We need them here and we need to bring them here. We shall need a great mass of shipping in 1942, far more than we can build ourselves, if we are to maintain and augment our war effort in the West and in the East.

These facts are, of course, all well known to the enemy, and we must therefore expect that Herr Hitler will do his utmost to prey upon our shipping and to reduce the volume of American supplies entering these islands. Having conquered France and Norway, his clutching fingers reach out on both sides of us into the ocean. I have never under-rated this danger, and you know I have never concealed it from you. Therefore, I hope you will believe me when I say that I have complete confidence in the Royal Navy, aided by the Air Force of the Coastal Command, and that in one way or another I am sure they will be able to meet every changing phase of this truly mortal struggle, and that sustained by the courage of our merchant seamen, and the dockers and workmen of all our ports, we shall outwit, out-manoeuvre, outfight and outlast the worst that the enemy's malice and ingenuity can contrive.

I have left the greatest issue to the end. You will have seen that Sir John Dill, our principal military adviser, the Chief of the Imperial General Staff, has warned us all that Hitler may be forced by the strategic, economic and political stresses in Europe, to try to invade these islands in the near future. That is a warning which no one should disregard. Naturally, we are working night and day to have everything ready. Of course, we are far stronger than we ever were before, incomparably stronger than we were in July, August and September. Our Navy is more powerful, our flotillas are more numerous; we are far stronger, actually and relatively, in the air above these islands, than we were when our Fighter Command beat off and beat down the Nazi attack last autumn. Our Army is more numerous, more mobile and far better equipped and trained than in September, and still more than in July.

I have the greatest confidence in our Commander-in-Chief, General Brooke, and in the generals of proved ability, who, under him, guard the different quarters of our land. But most of all I put my faith in the simple unaffected resolve to conquer or die which will animate and inspire nearly 4,000,000 Britons with serviceable weapons in their hands. It is not an easy military operation to invade an island like Great Britain, without the command of the sea and without the command of the air, and then to face what will be waiting for the invader here. But I must drop one word of caution; for next to cowardice and treachery, over-confidence, leading to neglect or slothfulness, is the worst of martial crimes. Therefore, I drop one word of caution. A Nazi invasion of Great Britain last autumn would have been a more or less improvised affair. Hitler took it for granted that when France gave in we should give in; but we did not give in. And he had to think again. An invasion now will be supported by a much more carefully prepared tackle and equipment of landing-craft and other apparatus, all of which will have been planned and manufactured in the winter months. We must all be prepared to meet gas attacks, parachute attacks and glider attacks, with constancy, forethought and practised skill.

I must again emphasize what General Dill has said, and what I pointed out myself last year. In order to win the war Hitler must destroy Great Britain. He may carry havoc into the Balkan States; he may tear great provinces out of Russia; he may march to the Caspian; he may march to the gates of India. All this will avail him nothing. It may spread his curse more widely throughout Europe and Asia, but it will not avert his doom. With every month that passes the many proud and once happy countries he is now holding down by brute force and vile intrigue are learning to hate the Prussian yoke and the Nazi name as nothing has ever been hated so fiercely and so widely among men before. And all the time, masters of the sea and air, the British Empire—nay, in a certain sense, the whole English-speaking world—will be on his track, bearing with them the swords of justice.

The other day, President Roosevelt gave his opponent in the late Presidential Election a letter of introduction to me, and in it he wrote out a verse, in his own hand-writing, from Longfellow which, he said, 'applies to you people as it does to us'. Here is the verse :

> . . . Sail on, O Ship of State !
> Sail on, O Union, strong and great !
> Humanity with all its fears,
> With all the hopes of future years,
> Is hanging breathless on thy fate !

What is the answer that I shall give, in your name, to this great man, the thrice-chosen head of a nation of 130,000,000 ? Here is the answer which I will give to President Roosevelt : Put your confidence in us. Give us your faith and your blessing, and, under Providence, all will be well.

We shall not fail or falter; we shall not weaken or tire. Neither the sudden shock of battle, nor the long-drawn trials of vigilance and exertion will wear us down. Give us the tools, and we will finish the job.

The War Speeches

Prime Minister to Sir Edward Bridges
and General Ismay   12.xi.40

The Prime Minister has noticed that the habit of private secretaries and others of addressing each other by their Christian names about matters of an official character is increasing, and ought to be stopped. The use of Christian names in inter-departmental correspondence should be confined only to brief explanatory covering notes or to purely personal and private explanations.

It is hard enough to follow people by their surnames.

Prime Minister to Minister of Food   March 21, '41

I hope the term 'Communal Feeding Centres' is not going to be adopted. It is an odious expression, suggestive of Communism and the workhouse. I suggest you call them 'British Restaurants'. Everybody associates the word 'restaurant' with a good meal, and they may as well have the name if they cannot get anything else.

Books in all their variety are often the means by which civilization may be carried triumphantly forward.

Except for our fighting services, we have been driven back to a large extent from the carnivore to the herbivore. That may be quite satisfactory to the dietetic scientists who would like to make us all live on nuts, but undoubtedly it has produced, and is producing, a very definite effect upon the energetic output of the heavy worker.

I was asked last week whether I was aware of some uneasiness which it was said existed in the country on account of the gravity, as it was described, of the war situation. So I thought it would be a good thing to go and see for myself what this 'uneasiness' amounted to, and I went to some of our great cities and seaports which had been most heavily bombed, and to some of the places where the poorest people had got it worst. I have come back not only reassured, but refreshed. To leave the offices in Whitehall with their ceaseless hum of activity and stress, and to go out to the front, by which I mean the streets and wharves of London or Liverpool, Manchester, Cardiff, Swansea or Bristol, is like going out of a hot-house on to the bridge of a fighting ship. It is a tonic which I should recommend any who are suffering from fretfulness to take in strong doses when they have need of it.

It is quite true that I have seen many painful scenes of havoc, and of fine buildings and acres of cottage homes blasted into rubble-heaps of ruin. But it is just in those very places where the malice of the savage enemy has done its worst, and where the ordeal of the men, women and children has been most severe, that I found their morale most high and splendid. Indeed, I felt encompassed by an exaltation of spirit in the people which seemed to lift mankind and its troubles above the level of material facts into that joyous serenity we think belongs to a better world than this.

Of their kindness to me I cannot speak, because I have never sought it or dreamed of it, and can never deserve it. I can only assure you that I and my colleagues, or comrades rather—for that is what they are—will toil with every scrap of life and strength, according to the lights that are granted to us, not to fail these people or be wholly unworthy of their faithful and generous regard. The British nation is stirred and moved as it has never been at any time in its long eventful, famous history, and it is no hackneyed trope of speech to say that they mean to conquer or to die.

What a triumph the life of these battered cities is, over the worst that fire and bomb can do. What a vindication of the civilized and decent way of living we have been trying to work for and work towards in our island. What a proof of the virtues of free institutions. What a test of the quality of our local authorities, and of institutions and customs and societies so steadily built. This ordeal by fire has even in a certain sense exhilarated the manhood and womanhood of Britain. The sublime but also terrible and sombre experiences and emotions of the battlefield which for centuries had been reserved for the soldiers and sailors, are now shared, for good or ill, by the entire population. All are proud to be under the fire of the enemy. Old men, little children, the crippled veterans of former wars, aged women, the ordinary hard-pressed citizen or subject of the King, as he likes to call himself, the sturdy workmen who swing the hammers or load the ships; skilful craftsmen; the members of every kind of ARP service, are proud to feel that they stand in the line together with our fighting men, when one of the greatest of causes is being fought out, as fought out it will be, to the end. This is indeed the grand heroic period of our history, and the light of glory shines on all.

You may imagine how deeply I feel my own responsibility to all these people; my responsibility to bear my part in bringing them safely out of this long, stern, scowling valley through which we are marching, and not to demand from them their sacrifices and exertions in vain.

During the last year we have gained by our bearing

and conduct a potent hold upon the sentiments of the people of the United States. Never, never in our history, have we been held in such admiration and regard across the Atlantic Ocean. In the great Republic, now in much travail and stress of soul, it is customary to use all the many valid, solid arguments about American interests and American safety, which depend upon the destruction of Hitler and his foul gang and even fouler doctrines. But in the long run—believe me, for I know—the action of the United States will be dictated, not by methodical calculations of profit and loss, but by moral sentiment, and by that gleaming flash of resolve which lifts the hearts of men and nations, and springs from the spiritual foundations of human life itself.

I turn aside from the stony path we have to tread, to indulge a moment of lighter relief. I dare say you have read in the newspapers that, by a special proclamation, the Italian Dictator has congratulated the Italian Army in Albania on the glorious laurels they have gained by their victory over the Greeks. Here surely is the world's record in the domain of the ridiculous and the contemptible. This whipped jackal, Mussolini, who to save his own skin has made all Italy a vassal state of Hitler's Empire, comes frisking up at the sides of the German tiger with yelpings not only of appetite—that can be understood—but even of triumph. Different things strike different people in different ways. But I am sure there are a great many millions in the British Empire and in the United States, who will find a new object in life in making sure that when we come to the final reckoning this absurd impostor will be abandoned to public justice and universal scorn.

No prudent and far-seeing man can doubt that the eventual and total defeat of Hitler and Mussolini is certain, in view of the respective declared resolves of the British and American democracies. There are less than 70,000,000 malignant Huns—some of whom are curable and others killable—many of whom are already engaged in holding down Austrians, Czechs, Poles, French, and the many other ancient races they now bully and pillage. The peoples of the British Empire and of the United States number nearly 200,000,000 in their homelands and in the British Dominions alone. They possess the unchallengeable command of the oceans, and will soon obtain decisive superiority in the air. They have more wealth, more technical resources, and they make more steel, than the whole of the rest of the world put together. They are determined that the cause of freedom shall not be trampled down, nor the tide of world progress turned backwards, by the criminal dictators.

While therefore we naturally view with sorrow and anxiety much that is happening in Europe and in Africa, and may happen in Asia, we must not lose our sense of proportion and thus become discouraged or alarmed. When we face with a steady eye the difficulties which lie before us, we may derive new confidence from remembering those we have already overcome. Nothing that is happening now is comparable in gravity with the dangers through which we passed last year. Nothing that can happen in the East is comparable with what is happening in the West.

Last time I spoke to you I quoted the lines of Longfellow which President Roosevelt had written out for me in his own hand. I have some other lines which are less well known but which seem apt and appropriate to our fortunes tonight, and I believe they will be so judged wherever the English language is spoken or the flag of freedom flies :

For while the tired waves, vainly breaking,
   Seem here no painful inch to gain,
Far back, through creeks and inlets making,
   Comes silent, flooding in, the main.

And not by eastern windows only,
   When daylight comes, comes in the light;
In front the sun climbs slow, how slowly!
   But westward, look, the land is bright.
                              A world broadcast, April 27, 1941

There is no operation in war more dangerous or more important than the conduct of a rear-guard action and the extrication of a rear-guard from difficult and broken country.

I could not resist paying my tribute to Rommel. 'We have a very daring and skilful opponent against us, and, if I may say across the havoc of war, a great general. . . .' My reference to Rommel passed off quite well at the moment. Later on I heard that some people had been offended. They could not feel that any virtue should be recognized in an enemy leader. This churlishness is a well-known streak in human nature, but contrary to the spirit in which a war is won, or a lasting peace established.

The Hinge of Fate, 'War Memoirs', Vol IV

An immense responsibility rests upon the German people for this subservience to the barbaric idea of autocracy. This is the gravamen [of the charge] against them in history—that, in spite of all their brains and courage, they worship Power, and let themselves be led by the nose.

It is a fine thing to be honest, but it is also very important to be right.

Generals are often prone, if they have the chance, to choose a setpiece battle, when all is ready, at their own selected moment, rather than to wear down the enemy by continued unspectacular fighting. They naturally prefer certainty to hazard. They forget that war never stops, but burns on from day to day with ever-changing results not only in one theatre but in all.

Some have compared Hitler's conquests with those of Napoleon. It may be that Spain and Russia will shortly furnish new chapters to that theme. It must be remembered, however, that Napoleon's armies carried with them the fierce, liberating and equalitarian winds of the French Revolution, whereas Hitler's Empire has nothing behind it but racial self-assertion, espionage, pillage, corruption and the Prussian boot. Yet Napoleon's Empire, with all its faults, and all its glories, fell, and flashed away like snow at Easter till nothing remained but His Majesty's ship *Bellerophon,* which awaited its suppliant refugee. So I derive confidence that the will-power of the House of Commons, once again will perform its liberating function and humbly exercise and execute a high purpose among men; and I say this with the more confidence because we are no longer a small island lost in the northern mists, but around us gather in proud array all the free nations of the British Empire, and this time from across the Atlantic Ocean the mighty Republic of the United States proclaims itself on our side, or at our side, or, at any rate, near our side.

In some quarters of the House, or at any rate among some Members, there is a very acute realization of the gravity of our problems and of our dangers. I have never underrated them. I feel we are fighting for life and survival from day to day and from hour to hour. But, believe me, Herr Hitler has his problems, too, and if we only remain united and strive our utmost to increase our exertions, and work like one great family, standing together and helping each other, as 5,000,000 families in Britain are doing today under the fire of the enemy, I cannot conceive how anyone can doubt that victory will crown the good cause we serve. Government and Parliament alike have to be worthy of the undaunted and unconquerable people who give us their trust and who give their country their all.

It is a year almost to a day since, in the crash of the disastrous Battle of France, His Majesty's present Administration was formed. Men of all parties, duly authorized by their parties, joined hands together to fight this business to the end. That was a dark hour, and little did we know what storms and perils lay before us, and little did Herr Hitler know, when in June 1940 he received the total capitulation of France and when he expected to be master of all Europe in a few weeks and the world in a few years, that ten months later, in May 1941, he would be appealing to the much-tried German people to prepare themselves for the war of 1942. When I look back on the perils which have been overcome, upon the great mountain waves through which the gallant ship has driven, when I remember all that has gone wrong, and remember also all that has gone right, I feel sure we have no need to fear the tempest. Let it roar, and let it rage. We shall come through.

House of Commons, May 7, 1941

Ah! foolish diligent Germans, working so hard, thinking so deeply . . . poring over long calculations, fuming in newly-found prosperity, discontented amid the splendour of mundane success, how many bulwarks to your peace and glory did you not, with your own hands, successively tear down!

The World Crisis

In the twenty-second month of the war against Nazism we meet here in this old Palace of St. James's, itself not unscarred by the fire of the enemy, in order to proclaim the high purposes and resolves of the lawful constitutional Governments of Europe whose countries have been overrun; and we meet here also to cheer the hopes of free men and free peoples throughout the world. Here before us on the table lie the title-deeds of ten nations or States whose soil has been invaded and polluted, and whose men, women and children lie prostrate or writhing under the Hitler yoke. But here also, duly authorized by the Parliament and democracy of Britain, are gathered the servants of the ancient British Monarchy and the accredited representatives of the British Dominions beyond the seas, of Canada, Australia, New Zealand and South Africa, of the Empire of India, of Burma and of our Colonies in every quarter of the globe. They have drawn their swords in this cause. They will never let them fall till life is gone or victory is won. Here we meet, while from across the Atlantic Ocean the hammers and lathes of the United States signal in a rising hum their message of encouragement and their promise of swift and evergrowing aid.

What tragedies, what horrors, what crimes have Hitler and all that Hitler stands for brought upon Europe and the world! The ruins of Warsaw, of Rotterdam, of Belgrade are monuments which will long recall to future generations the outrage of the unopposed air-bombing applied with calculated scientific cruelty to helpless populations. Here in London and throughout the cities of our island, and in Ireland, there may also be seen the marks of devastation. They are being repaid, and presently they will be more than repaid.

But far worse than these visible injuries is the misery of the conquered peoples. We see them hounded, terrorized, exploited. Their manhood by the million is forced to work under conditions indistinguishable in many cases from actual slavery. Their goods and chattels are pillaged, or filched for worthless money. Their homes, their daily life are pried into and spied upon by the all-pervading system of secret political police which, having reduced the Germans themselves to abject docility, now stalk the streets and byways of a dozen lands. Their religious faiths are affronted, persecuted or oppressed in the interests of a fantastic paganism devised to perpetuate the worship and sustain the tyranny of one abominable creature. Their traditions, their culture, their laws, their institutions, social and political alike, are suppressed by force or undermined by subtle, coldly-planned intrigue.

The prisons of the Continent no longer suffice. The concentration camps are overcrowded. Every dawn the German volleys crack. Czechs, Poles, Dutchmen, Norwegians, Yugoslavs and Greeks, Frenchmen, Belgians, Luxembourgers, make the great sacrifice for faith and country. A vile race of quislings—to use the new word which will carry the scorn of mankind down the centuries—is hired to fawn upon the conqueror, to collaborate in his designs, and to enforce his rule upon their fellow-countrymen, while grovelling low themselves. Such is the plight of once-glorious Europe, and such are the atrocities against which we are in arms.

It is upon this foundation that Hitler, with his tattered lackey Mussolini at his tail and Admiral Darlan frisking by his side, pretends to build out of hatred, appetite and racial assertion a new order for Europe. Never did so mocking a fantasy obsess the mind of mortal man. We cannot tell what the course of this fell war will be as it spreads remorseless through ever-wider regions. We know it will be hard, we expect it will be long; we cannot predict or measure its episodes or its tribulations. But one thing is certain, one thing is sure, one thing stands out stark and undeniable, massive and unassailable, for all the world to see.

It will not be by German hands that the structure of Europe will be rebuilt or the union of the European family achieved. In every country into which the German armies and the Nazi police have broken there has sprung up from the soil a hatred of the German name and a contempt for the Nazi creed which the passage of hundreds of years will not efface from human memory. We cannot yet see how deliverance will come, or when it will come, but nothing is more certain than that every trace of Hitler's footsteps, every stain of his infected and corroding fingers will be sponged and purged and, if need be, blasted from the surface of the earth.

We are here to affirm and fortify our union in that ceaseless and unwearying effort which must be made if the captive peoples are to be set free. A year ago His Majesty's Government was left alone to face the storm, and to many of our friends and enemies alike it may have seemed that our days too were numbered, and that Britain and its institutions would sink for ever beneath the verge. But I may with some pride remind your Excellencies that, even in that dark hour when our Army was disorganized and almost weaponless, when scarcely a gun or a tank remained in Britain, when almost all our stores and ammunition had been lost in France, never for one moment did the British people dream of making peace with the conqueror, and never for a moment did they despair of the common cause. On the contrary, we proclaimed at that very time to all men, not only to ourselves, our determination not to make peace until every one of the ravaged and enslaved countries was liberated and until the Nazi domination was broken and destroyed.

See how far we have travelled since those breathless days of June a year ago. Our solid, stubborn strength has stood the awful test. We are masters of our own air, and now reach out in ever-growing retribution upon the enemy. The Royal Navy holds the seas. The Italian Fleet cowers diminished in harbour, the German Navy is largely crippled or sunk. The murderous raids upon our ports, cities and factories have been powerless to quench the spirit of the British nation, to stop our national life, or check the immense expansion of our war industry. The food and arms from across the oceans are coming safely in. Full provision to replace all sunken tonnage is being made here, and still more by our friends in the United States. We are becoming an armed community. Our land forces are being perfected in equipment and training.

Hitler may turn and trample this way and that through tortured Europe. He may spread his course far and wide, and carry his curse with him: he may break into Africa or into Asia. But it is here, in this island fortress, that he will have to reckon in the end. We shall strive to resist by land and sea. We shall be on his track wherever he goes. Our air-power will continue to teach the German homeland that war is not all loot and triumph.

We shall aid and stir the people of every conquered country to resistance and revolt. We shall break up and derange every effort which Hitler makes to systematize and consolidate his subjugation. He will find no peace, no rest, no halting-place, no parley. And if, driven to desperate hazards, he attempts the invasion of the British Isles, as well he may, we shall not flinch from the supreme trial. With the help of God, of which we must all feel daily conscious, we shall continue steadfast in faith and duty till our task is done.

This, then, is the message which we send forth today to all the States and nations bond or free, to all the men in all the lands who care for freedom's cause, to our allies and well-wishers in Europe, to our American friends and helpers drawing ever closer in their might across the ocean : this is the message—Lift up your hearts. All will come right. Out of the depths of sorrow and sacrifice will be born again the glory of mankind.

Speech to Dominion High Commissioners,

June 12, 1941

I am grateful, President Valentine, for the honour which you have conferred upon me in making me a Doctor of Laws of Rochester University in the State of New York. I am extremely complimented by the expressions of praise and commendation in which you have addressed me, not becase I am or ever can be worthy of them, but because they are an expression of American confidence and affection which I shall ever strive to deserve.

But what touches me most in this ceremony is that sense of kinship and of unity which I feel exists between us this afternoon. As I speak from Downing Street to

Rochester University and through you to the people of the United States, I almost feel I have the right to do so, because my mother, as you have stated, was born in your city, and here my grandfather, Leonard Jerome, lived for so many years, conducting as a prominent and rising citizen a newspaper with the excellent eighteenth-century title of the Plain Dealer.

The great Burke has truly said, 'People will not look forward to posterity who never look backward to their ancestors', and I feel it most agreeable to recall to you that the Jeromes were rooted for many generations in American soil, and fought in Washington's armies for the independence of the American Colonies and the foundation of the United States. I expect I was on both sides then. And I may say I feel on both sides of the Atlantic Ocean now.

At intervals during the last forty years I have addressed scores of great American audiences in almost every part of the Union. I have learnt to admire the courtesy of these audiences; their sense of fair play; their sovereign sense of humour, never minding the joke that is turned against themselves; their earnest, voracious desire to come to the root of the matter and to be well and truly informed on Old World affairs.

And now, in this time of world storm, when I have been called upon by King and Parliament and with the support of all parties in the State to bear the chief responsibility in Great Britain, and when I have had the supreme honour of speaking for the British nation in its most deadly danger and in its finest hour, it has given me comfort and inspiration to feel that I think as you do, that our hands are joined across the oceans, and that our pulses throb and beat as one. Indeed, I will make so bold as to say that here at least, in my mother's birth city of Rochester, I hold a latchkey to American hearts.

Strong tides of emotion, fierce surges of passion, sweep the broad expanses of the Union in this year of fate. In that prodigious travail there are many elemental forces, there is much heart-searching and self-questioning; some pangs, some sorrow, some conflict of voices, but no fear. The world is witnessing the birth throes of a sublime resolve. I shall presume to confess to you that I have no doubts what that resolve will be. The whole stature of man, his genius, his initiative and his nobility, is ground down under systems of mechanical barbarism and of organized and scheduled terror.

For more than a year we British have stood alone, uplifted by your sympathy and respect and sustained by our own unconquerable willpower and by the increasing growth and hopes of your massive aid. In these British Islands that look so small upon the map we stand, the faithful guardians of the rights and dearest hopes of a dozen States and nations now gripped and tormented in a base and cruel servitude. Whatever happens we shall endure to the end.

But what is the explanation of the enslavement of Europe by the German Nazi regime? How did they do it? It is but a few years ago since one united gesture by the peoples, great and small, who are now broken in the dust, would have warded off from mankind the fearful ordeal it has had to undergo. But there was no unity. There was no vision. The nations were pulled down one by one while the others gaped and chattered. One by one, each in his turn, they let themselves be caught. One after another they were felled by brutal violence or poisoned from within by subtle intrigue.

And now the old lion with her lion cubs at her side stands alone against hunters who are armed with deadly

186

weapons and impelled by desperate and destructive rage. Is the tragedy to repeat itself once more? Ah no! This is not the end of the tale. The stars in their courses proclaim the deliverance of mankind. Not so easily shall the onward progress of the peoples be barred. Not so easily shall the lights of freedom die.

But time is short. Every month that passes adds to the length and to the perils of the journey that will have to be made. United we stand. Divided we fall. Divided, the dark age returns. United, we can save and guide the world.

Broadcast to America, June 16, 1941

Personally, I like short words and vulgar fractions.
Speech at Margate, October 10, 1953

A single glass of champagne imparts a feeling of exhilaration. The nerves are braced; the imagination is agreeably stirred; the wits become more nimble. A bottle produces a contrary effect. Excess causes a comatose insensibility. So it is with war; and the quality of both is best discovered by sipping.

I have taken occasion to speak to you tonight because we have reached one of the climacterics of the war. The first of these intense turning-points was a year ago when France fell prostrate under the German hammer, and when we had to face the storm alone. The second was when the Royal Air Force beat the Hun raiders out of the daylight air, and thus warded off the Nazi invasion of our island while we were still ill-armed and ill-prepared. The third turning-point was when the President and Congress of the United States passed the Lease-and-Lend enactment, devoting nearly 2,000 millions sterling of the wealth of the New World to help us to defend our liberties and their own. Those were the three climacterics. The fourth is now upon us.

At four o'clock this morning Hitler attacked and invaded Russia. All his usual formalities of perfidy were observed with scrupulous technique. A non-aggression treaty had been solemnly signed and was in force between the two countries. No complaint had been made by Germany of its non-fulfilment. Under its cloak of false confidence, the German armies drew up in immense strength along a line which stretches from the White Sea to the Black Sea; and their air fleets and armoured divisions slowly and methodically took their stations. Then, suddenly, without declaration of war, without even an ultimatum, German bombs rained down from the air upon the Russian cities, the German troops violated the frontiers; and an hour later the German Ambassador, who till the night before was lavishing his assurances of friendship, almost of alliance, upon the Russians, called upon the Russian Foreign Minister to tell him that a state of war existed between Germany and Russia.

Thus was repeated on a far larger scale the same kind of outrage against every form of signed compact and international faith which we have witnessed in Norway, Denmark, Holland and Belgium, and which Hitler's accomplice and jackal Mussolini so faithfully imitated in the case of Greece.

All this was no surprise to me. In fact I gave clear and precise warnings to Stalin of what was coming. I gave him warning as I have given warning to others before. I can only hope that this warning did not fall unheeded. All we know at present is that the Russian people are defending their native soil and that their leaders have called upon them to resist to the utmost.

Hitler is a monster of wickedness, insatiable in his lust for blood and plunder. Not content with having all Europe under his heel, or else terrorized into various forms of abject submission, he must now carry his work of butchery and desolation among the vast multitudes of Russia and of Asia. The terrible military machine, which we and the rest of the civilized world so foolishly, so supinely, so insensately allowed the Nazi gangsters to build up year by year from almost nothing, cannot stand idle lest it rust or fall to pieces. It must be in continual motion, grinding up human lives and trampling down the homes and the rights of hundreds of millions of men. Moreover it must be fed, not only with flesh but with oil.

So now this bloodthirsty guttersnipe must launch his mechanized armies upon new fields of slaughter, pillage and devastation. Poor as are the Russian peasants, workmen and soldiers, he must steal from them their daily bread; he must devour their harvests; he must rob them of the oil which drives their ploughs; and thus produce a famine without example in human history. And even the carnage and ruin which his victory, should he gain it—he has not gained it yet—will bring upon the Russian people, will itself be only a stepping-stone to the attempt to plunge the 400,000,000 or 500,000,000 who live in China, and the 350,000,000 who live in India, into that bottomless pit of human degradation over which the diabolic emblem of the Swastika flaunts itself. It is not too much to say here this summer evening that the lives and happiness of 1,000,000,000 additional people are now menaced with brutal Nazi violence. That is enough to make us hold our breath. But presently I shall show you something else that lies behind, and something that touches very nearly the life of Britain and of the United States.

The Nazi regime is indistinguishable from the worst features of Communism. It is devoid of all theme and principle except appetite and racial domination. It excels all forms of human wickedness in the efficiency of its cruelty and ferocious aggression. No one has been a more consistent opponent of Communism than I have for the last twenty-five years. I will unsay no word that I have spoken about it. But all this fades away before the spectacle which is now unfolding. The past with its crimes, its follies and its tragedies, flashes away. I see the Russian soldiers standing on the threshold of their native land, guarding the fields which their fathers have tilled from time immemorial. I see them guarding their homes where mothers and wives pray—ah yes, for there are times when all pray—for the safety of their loved ones, the return of the bread-winner, of their champion, of their protector. I see the 10,000 villages of Russia, where the means of existence was wrung so hardly from the soil, but where there are still primordial human joys, where maidens laugh and children play. I see advancing upon all this in hideous onslaught the Nazi war machine, with its clanking, heel-clicking, dandified Prussian officers, its crafty expert agents fresh from the cowing and tying-down of a dozen countries. I see also the dull, drilled, docile, brutish masses of the Hun soldiery plodding on like a swarm of crawling locusts. I see the German bombers and fighters in the sky, still smarting from many a British whipping, delighted to find what they believe is an easier and a safer prey.

Behind all this glare, behind all this storm, I see that small group of villainous men who plan, organize and launch this cataract of horrors upon mankind. And then my mind goes back across the years to the days when the Russian armies were our allies against the same deadly foe; when they fought with so much valour and constancy, and helped to gain a victory, a share in which, alas, they were—through no fault of ours—utterly cut off. I have lived through all this, and you will pardon me if I express my feelings and the stir of old memories.

But now I have to declare the decision of His Majesty's Government—and I feel sure it is a decision in which the great Dominions will, in due course, concur—for we must speak out now at once, without a day's delay. I have to make the declaration, but can you doubt what our policy will be? We have but one aim and one single, irrevocable purpose. We are resolved to destroy Hitler and every vestige of the Nazi regime. From this nothing will turn us—nothing. We will never parley, we will never negotiate with Hitler or any of his gang. We shall fight him by land, we shall fight him by sea, we shall fight him in the air, until with God's help we have rid the earth of his shadow and liberated its peoples from his yoke. Any man or State who fights on against Nazidom will have our aid. Any man or State who marches with Hitler is our foe. This applies not only to organized States but to all representatives of that vile race of quislings who make themselves the tools and agents of the Nazi regime against their fellow-countrymen and the lands of their birth. They—these quislings —like the Nazi leaders themselves, if not disposed of by their fellow-countrymen, which would save trouble, will be delivered by us on the morrow of victory to the justice of the Allied tribunals. That is our policy and that is our declaration. It follows, therefore, that we shall give whatever help we can to Russia and the Russian people. We shall appeal to all our friends and allies in every part of the world to take the same course and pursue it, as we shall, faithfully and steadfastly to the end.

We have offered the Government of Soviet Russia any technical or economic assistance which is in our power, and which is likely to be of service to them. We shall bomb Germany by day as well as by night in ever-increasing measure, casting upon them month by month a heavier discharge of bombs, and making the German people taste and gulp each month a sharper dose of the miseries they have showered upon mankind. It is noteworthy that only yesterday the Royal Air Force, fighting inland over French territory, cut down with very small loss to themselves twenty-eight of the Hun fighting machines in the air above the French soil they have invaded, defiled and profess to hold. But this is only a beginning. From now forward the main expansion of our Air Force proceeds with gathering speed. In another six months the weight of the help we are receiving from the United States in war materials of all kinds, and especially in heavy bombers, will begin to tell.

This is no class war, but a war in which the whole British Empire and Commonwealth of Nations is engaged without distinction of race, creed or party. It is not for me to speak of the action of the United States, but this I will say : if Hitler imagines that his attack on Soviet Russia will cause the slightest division of aims or slackening of effort in the great democracies who are resolved upon his doom, he is woefully mistaken. On the contrary, we shall be fortified and encouraged in our efforts to rescue mankind from his tyranny. We shall be strengthened and not weakened in determination and in resources.

This is no time to moralize on the follies of countries and Governments which have allowed themselves to be struck down one by one, when by united action they could have saved themselves and saved the world from this catastrophe. But when I spoke a few minutes ago of Hitler's blood-lust and the hateful appetites which have impelled or lured him on his Russian adventure, I said there was one deeper motive behind his outrage. He wishes to destroy the Russian power because he hopes that if he succeeds in this, he will be able to bring back to the main strength of his Army and Air Force from the East and hurl it upon this island, which he knows he must conquer or suffer the penalty of his crimes. His invasion of Russia is no more than a prelude to an attempted invasion of the British Isles. He hopes, no doubt, that all this may be accomplished before the winter comes, and that he can overwhelm Great Britain before the Fleet and airpower of the United States may intervene. He hopes that he may once again repeat, upon a greater scale than ever before, that process of destroying his enemies one by one, by which he has so long thrived and prospered, and that then the scene will be clear for the final act, without which all his conquests would be in vain—namely, the subjugation of the Western Hemisphere to his will and to his system.

The Russian danger is therefore our danger, and the danger of the United States, just as the cause of any Russian fighting for his hearth and home is the cause of free men and free peoples in every quarter of the globe. Let us learn the lessons already taught by such cruel experience. Let us redouble our exertions, and strike with united strength while life and power remain.

World broadcast, July 22, 1941

As to complacency, let me say this. Do not let anyone suppose that inside this enormous Government we are a mutual admiration society. I do not think, and my colleagues will bear me witness, any expression of scorn or severity which I have heard used by our critics, has come anywhere near the language I have been myself accustomed to use, not only orally, but in a continued stream of written minutes. In fact, I wonder that a great many of my colleagues are on speaking terms with me. They would not be if I had not complained of and criticized all evenly and alike. But, bound together as we are by a common purpose, the men who have joined hands in this affair put up with a lot, and I hope they will put up with a lot more. It is the duty of the Prime Minister to use the power which Parliament and the nation have given him to drive others, and in war like this that power has to be used irrespective of anyone's feelings. If we win, nobody will care. If we lose, there will be nobody to care.

House of Commons, June 25, 1941

It is not given to the cleverest and the most calculating of mortals to know with certainty what is their interest. Yet it is given to quite a lot of simple folk to know every day what is their duty.

We have all heard of how Dr. Guillotine was executed by the instrument he invented . . .
[Sir H. Samuel : he was not.]
Well, he ought to have been.

I remember one winter evening travelling to a railway station—which still worked—on my way north to visit troops. It was cold and raining. Darkness had almost fallen on the blacked-out streets. I saw everywhere long queues of people, among them hundreds of young girls in their silk stockings and high-heeled shoes, who had worked hard all day and were waiting for bus after bus, which came by already overcrowded, in the hope of reaching their homes for the night. When at that moment the doleful wail of the siren betokened the approach of the German bombers, I confess to you that my heart bled for London and the Londoners.

All this sort of thing went on for more than four months with hardly any intermission. I used to hold meetings of my Ministerial colleagues and members of the authorities concerned every week in Downing Street in order to check up and see how we stood. Sometimes the gas had failed over large areas—the only means of cooking for great numbers of people; sometimes the electricity. There were grievous complaints about the shelters and about conditions in them. Water was cut off, railways were cut or broken, large districts were destroyed by fire, 20,000 people were killed, and many more thousands were wounded.

But there was one thing about which there was never any doubt. The courage, the unconquerable grit and stamina of the Londoners showed itself from the very outset. Without that all would have failed. Upon that rock, all stood unshakable. All the public services were carried on, and all the intricate arrangements, far-reaching details, involving the daily lives of so many millions, were carried out, improvised, elaborated and perfected in the very teeth of the cruel and devastating storm.

County Council luncheon, July 14, 1941

Prime Minister to Foreign Office   August 27, 1941

Give me in a few lines the reasons which led to Siam calling itself Thailand. What are the historic merits of these two names?

We have to reckon with a criminal who by a mere gesture has decreed the death of 3,000,000 or 4,000,000 Russian and German soldiers. We stand here still the champions. If we fail, all fails, and if we fall, all will fall together. It is only by a superb, intense and prolonged effort of the whole British Empire that the great combination of about three-quarters of the human race against Nazidom will come into vehement and dynamic life. For more than a year we have been all alone : all alone, we have had to guard the treasure of mankind. Although there have been profound and encouraging changes in the situation, our own vital and commanding responsibilities remain undiminished; and we shall discharge them only by continuing to pour out in the common cause the utmost endeavours of our strength and virtue, and, if need be, to proffer the last drop of our heart's blood.

House of Commons, July 29, 1941

Canada is the linchpin of the English-speaking world. Canada, with those relations of friendly, affectionate intimacy with the United States on the one hand and with her unswerving fidelity to the British Commonwealth and the Motherland on the other, is the link which joins together these great branches of the human family, a link which, spanning the oceans, brings the continents into their true relation and will prevent in future generations any growth of division between the proud and the happy nations of Europe and the great countries which have come into existence in the New World.

The foundation of all democracy is that the people have the right to vote. To deprive them of that right is to make a mockery of all the high-sounding phrases which are so often used. At the bottom of all the tributes paid to democracy is the little man, walking into the little booth, with a little pencil, making a little cross on

a little bit of paper—no amount of rhetoric or volu-
minous discussion can possibly diminish the overwhelming importance of that point. The people have the right
to choose representatives in accordance with their wishes
and feelings.

House of Commons, October 31, 1944

Thus far then have we travelled along the terrible
road we chose at the call of duty. The mood of Britain
is wisely and rightly averse from every form of shallow
or premature exultation. This is no time for boasts or
glowing prophecies, but there is this—a year ago our
position looked forlorn and well-nigh desperate to all
eyes but our own. Today we may say aloud before an
awe-struck world, 'We are still masters of our fate. We
still are captain of our souls.'

House of Commons, September 9, 1941

Making allowance for the increase of population, we
have, in the 26th month of this war, reached, and in
some ways surpassed, the deployment of national effort
at home which after all the slaughter was not reached
until the 48th month of the last war. We cannot rest
content with that, and if Parliament, by patriotic and
constructive counsel, and without unduly harassing those
who bear the load, can stimulate and accelerate our
further advance, the House of Commons will be playing
its part, unyielding, persevering, indomitable, in the
overthrow of another Continental tyranny as in the
olden times.

House of Commons, November 12, 1941

As soon as I heard, last night, that Japan had attacked
the United States, I felt it necessary that Parliament
should be immediately summoned. It is indispensable to

our system of government that Parliament should play its full part in all the important acts of State and at all the crucial moments of the war; and I am glad to see that so many Members have been able to be in their places, despite the shortness of the notice. With the full approval of the nation, and of the Empire, I pledged the word of Great Britain, about a month ago, that should the United States be involved in war with Japan, a British declaration of war would follow within the hour. I therefore spoke to President Roosevelt on the Atlantic telephone last night, with a view to arranging the timing of our respective declarations. The President told me that he would this morning send a message to Congress, which, of course, as is well known, can alone make a declaration of war on behalf of the United States, and I then assured him that we would follow immediately.

However, it soon appeared that British territory in Malaya had also been the object of Japanese attack, and later on it was announced from Tokyo that the Japanese High Command—a curious form; not the Imperial Japanese Government—had declared that a state of war existed with Great Britain and the United States. That being so, there was no need to wait for the declaration by Congress.

American time is very nearly six hours behind ours. The Cabinet, therefore, which met at 12.30 today, authorized an immediate declaration of war upon Japan. Instructions were sent to His Majesty's Ambassador at Tokyo, and a communication was dispatched to the Japanese Chargé d'Affaires at 1 o'clock today to this effect :

Foreign Office, December 8

Sir,

On the evening of December 7 His Majesty's Government in the United Kingdom learned that Japanese forces, without previous warning either in the form of a declaration of war or of an ultimatum with a conditional declaration of war, had attempted a landing on the coast of Malaya and bombed Singapore and Hong Kong.

In view of these wanton acts of unprovoked aggression, committed in flagrant violation of international law, and particularly of Article 1 of the Third Hague Convention, relative to the opening of hostilities, to which both Japan and the United Kingdom are parties, His Majesty's Ambassador at Tokyo has been instructed to inform the Imperial Japanese Government, in the name of His Majesty's Government in the United Kingdom, that a state of war exists between the two countries.

I have the honour to be, with high consideration,

Sir,

Your obedient servant,

Winston S. Churchill

Meanwhile, hostilities had already begun. The Japanese began a landing in British territory in Northern Malaya at about 6 o'clock—1 a.m. local time—yesterday, and they were immediately engaged by our Forces, which were in readiness. The Home Office measures against Japanese nationals were set in motion at 10.45 last night. The House will see, therefore, that no time has been lost, and that we are actually ahead of our engagements.

Now that the issue is joined in the most direct manner, it only remains for the two great democracies to face their task with whatever strength God may give them.

It is of the highest importance that there should be no underrating of the gravity of the new dangers we have to meet, either here or in the United States. The enemy has attacked with an audacity which may spring from recklessness, but which may also spring from a conviction of strength. The ordeal to which the English-speaking world and our heroic Russian allies are being exposed will certainly be hard, especially at the outset, and will probably be long, yet when we look around us over the sombre panorama of the world, we have no reason to doubt the justice of our cause or that our strength and will-power will be sufficient to sustain it. We have at least four-fifths of the population of the globe upon our side.

We are responsible for their safety and for their future. In the past we have had a light which flickered, in the present we have a light which flames, and in the future there will be a light which shines over all the land and sea.

Mr. Churchill repeated this speech on the radio the same evening, and added this appeal to munition workers :

It is particularly necessary that all munitions workers and those engaged in war industries should make a further effort proportionate to the magnitude of our perils and the magnitude of our cause. Particularly does this apply to tanks and, above all, to aircraft. Aircraft will be more than ever necessary now that the war has spread over so many wide spaces of the earth. I appeal to all those in the factories to do their utmost to make sure that we make an extra contribution to the general resources of the great alliance of free peoples that has been hammered and forged into strength amidst the fire of war.

A speech delivered first to the House of Commons and then broadcast to the world, December 8, 1941

I feel greatly honoured that you should have invited me to enter the United States Senate Chamber and address the representatives of both branches of Congress. The fact that my American forebears have for so many generations played their part in the life of the United States, and that here I am, an Englishman, welcomed in your midst, makes this experience one of the most moving and thrilling in my life, which is already long and has not been entirely uneventful. I wish indeed that my mother, whose memory I cherish across the vale of years, could have been here to see. By the way, I cannot help reflecting that if my father had been American and my mother British, instead of the other way round, I might have got here on my own. In that case, this would not have been the first time you would have heard my voice. In that case I should not have needed any invitation, but if I had, it is hardly likely it would have been unanimous. So perhaps things are better as they are. I may confess, however, that I do not feel quite like a fish out of water in a legislative assembly where English is spoken.

I am a child of the House of Commons. I was brought up in my father's house to believe in democracy. 'Trust the people'—that was his message. I used to see him cheered at meetings and in the streets by crowds of working men way back in those aristocratic Victorian days when, as Disraeli said, the world was for the few, and for the very few. Therefore I have been in full harmony all my life with the tides which have flowed on both sides of the Atlantic against privilege and monopoly, and I have steered confidently towards the Gettysburg ideal of 'government of the people by the people for the people'. I owe my advancement entirely to the House of Commons, whose servant I am. In my country, as in yours, public men are proud to be the servants of the

State and would be ashamed to be its masters. On any day, if they thought the people wanted it, the House of Commons could by a simple vote remove me from my office. But I am not worrying about it at all. As a matter of fact, I am sure they will approve very highly of my journey here, for which I obtained the King's permission in order to meet the President of the United States and to arrange with him all that mapping-out of our military plans, and for all those intimate meetings of the high officers of the armed services of both countries, which are indispensable to the successful prosecution of the war.

I should like to say first of all how much I have been impressed and encouraged by the breadth of view and sense of proportion which I have found in all quarters over here to which I have had access. Anyone who did not understand the size and solidity of the foundations of the United States might easily have expected to find an excited, disturbed, self-centred atmosphere, with all minds fixed upon the novel, startling and painful episodes of sudden war as they hit America. After all, the United States have been attacked and set upon by three most powerfully-armed dictator States. The greatest military power in Europe, the greatest military power in Asia, Germany and Japan, Italy, too, have all declared, and are making, war upon you, and a quarrel is opened, which can only end in their overthrow or yours. But here in Washington, in these memorable days, I have found an Olympian fortitude which, far from being based upon complacency, is only the mask of an inflexible purpose and the proof of a sure and well-grounded confidence in the final outcome. We in Britain had the same feeling in our darkest days. We, too, were sure in the end all would be well. You do not, I am certain underrate the severity of the ordeal to which you and we have still to be subjected. The forces ranged against us are enormous. They are bitter, they are ruthless. The wicked men and their factions who have launched their peoples on the path of war and conquest know that they will be called to terrible account if they cannot beat down by force of arms the peoples they have assailed. They will stop at nothing. They have a vast accumulation of war weapons of all kinds. They have highly-trained, disciplined armies, navies and air services. They have plans and designs which have long been tried and matured. They will stop at nothing that violence or treachery can suggest. . . . Some people may be startled or momentarily depressed when, like your President, I speak of a long and hard war. But our peoples would rather know the truth, sombre though it be. And after all, when we are doing the noblest work in the world, not only defending our hearths and homes but the cause of freedom in other lands, the question of whether deliverance comes in 1942, 1943 or 1944 falls into its proper place in the grand proportions of human history. Sure I am that this day—now—we are the masters of our fate; that the task which has been set us is not above our strength; that its pangs and toils are not beyond our endurance. As long as we have faith in our cause and an unconquerable will-power, salvation will not be denied us. In the words of the Psalmist, 'He shall not be afraid of evil tidings; his heart is fixed, trusting in the Lord.' Not all the tidings will be evil. . . .

An Address to the Senate and the House of Representatives in the Senate Chamber at Washington and broadcast to the world, December 26, 1941

. . . This is a very hard war. Its numerous and fearful problems reach down to the very foundations of human society. Its scope is world wide, and it involves all nations and every man, woman and child in them. Strategy and economics are interwoven. Sea, land, and air are but a single service. The latest refinements of science are linked with the cruelties of the Stone Age. The workshop and the fighting line are one. All may fall, all will stand together. We must aid each other, we must stand by each other.

We must confront our perils and trials with that national unity which cannot be broken, and a national force which is inexhaustible. We must confront them with resilience and ingenuity which are fearless, and above all with that inflexible will-power to endure and yet to dare for which our island race has long been renowned. Thus, and thus alone, can we be worthy champions of that grand alliance of nearly thirty States and nations which without our resistance would never have come into being, but which now has only to march on together until tyranny is trampled down. . . .

March 26, 1942

. . . Here in the thirty-third month of the war none of us is weary of the struggle, none of us is calling for any favours from the enemy. If he plays rough we can play rough too. Whatever we have got to take we will take, and we will give it back in even greater measure. When we began this war we were a peaceful and unarmed people. We had striven hard for peace. We had gone into folly over our desire for peace and the enemy started all primed-up and ready to strike. But now, as the months go by and the great machine keeps turning and the labour becomes skilled and habituated to its task, we are going to be the ones who have the modern scientific tackle. It is not now going to be a fight of brave men against men armed. It is going to be a fight on our side of people who have not only the resolve and the cause, but who also have the weapons.

We shall go forward together. The road upwards is stony. There are upon our journey dark and dangerous valleys through which we have to make and fight our way. But it is sure and certain that if we persevere—and we shall persevere—we shall come through these dark and dangerous valleys into a sunlight broader and more genial and more lasting than mankind has ever known . . .

Speech at Leeds, May 16, 1942

I am not going to express any opinion about what is going to happen. I cannot tell the House—and the enemy—what reinforcements are at hand, or are approaching, or when they will arrive. I have never made any predictions, except things like saying that Singapore would hold out. What a fool and a knave I should have been to say that it would fall! I have not made any arrogant, confident boasting predictions at all. On the contrary, I have stuck hard to my 'blood, toil, tears and sweat', to which I have added muddle and mis-management, and that, to some extent I must admit, is what you have got out of it . . .

House of Commons, July 2, 1942

Egypt is already clear of the enemy; we are advancing into Cyrenaica, and we may rely upon our generals and upon the Air Force to accomplish amazing feats now that the main force of the enemy has been broken and they have before them the opportunity of regaining in a few weeks, perhaps in much less than that, ground which otherwise might have taken long campaigns to reconquer. Taken by itself, the Battle of Egypt must be regarded as an historic British victory. In order to celebrate it directions are being given to ring the bells throughout the land next Sunday morning, and I should think that many will listen to their peals with thankful hearts. The time will be notified through the agency of the BBC, for everyone's convenience, and also to explain that the bells are not being rung on account of invasion.

House of Commons speech, November 11, 1942

I have thought in this difficult period, when so much fighting and so many critical and complicated manoeuvres are going on, that it is above all things important that our policy and conduct should be upon the highest level, and that honour should be our guide.

. . . As I flew back to Cairo across the vast spaces, back across the Caspian Sea and the mountain ranges and deserts, I bore with me the conviction that in the British Empire, the United States and the Soviet Union, Hitler has forged an alliance of partnership which is strong enough to beat him to the ground and steadfast enough to persevere, not only until his wickedness has been punished, but until some at least of the ruin he has wrought has been repaired.

We have recently been reminded that the third anniversary of the war has come and gone, and that we are now entered upon the fourth year. We are indeed entitled, nay, bound, to be thankful for the inestimable and measureless improvements in our position which have marked the last two years. From being all alone, the sole champion left in arms against Nazi tyranny, we are now among the leaders of a majestic company of States and nations, including the greatest nations of the world, the United States and Russia, all moving forward together until absolute victory is won, and not only won but established upon unshakeable foundations. In spite of all the disappointing episodes, disasters and sufferings through which we have passed, our strength has grown without halt or pause, and we can see each day that not only our own power but the weight of the United States becomes increasingly effective in the struggle.

Apart from the physical and moral dangers of the war through which we have made our way so far without serious injury, there was a political danger which at one time seemed to me, at any rate, to be a formidable threat. After the collapse of France, when the German armies strode on irresistibly in triumph and conquest, there seemed to be a possibility that Hitler might establish himself as a kind of Charlemagne in Europe, and would unite many countries under German sway, while at the same time pointing to our island as the author of the blockade and the cause of all their woes. That danger, such as it was, and I certainly did not think it negligible, has rolled away. The German is now more hated in every country in Europe than any race has been since human records began. In a dozen countries Hitler's firing-parties are at work every morning, and a dark stream of blood flows between the Germans and almost all their fellow men. The cruelties, the massacres of hostages, the brutal persecutions in which the Germans have indulged in every land into which their armies have broken have recently received an addition in the most bestial, the most squalid and the most senseless of all their offences, namely, the mass deportation of Jews from France, with the pitiful horrors attendant upon the calculated and final scattering of families. This tragedy fills one with astonishment as well as with indignation, and it illustrates as nothing else can the utter degradation of the Nazi nature and theme, and the degradation of all who lend themselves to its unnatural and perverted passions.

When the hour of liberation strikes in Europe, as strike it will, it will also be the hour of retribution. I wish most particularly to identify His Majesty's Government and the House of Commons with the solemn words which were used lately by the President of the United States, namely, that those who are guilty of the Nazi crimes will have to stand up before tribunals in every land where their atrocities have been committed in order that an indelible warning may be given to future ages, and that successive generations of men may say, 'So perish all who do the like again.'

House of Commons, September 8, 1942

Prime Minister to Lord Cherwell   March 10, 1942

I agree with the general outline of your minute (about further restriction of civil consumption). In particular I am opposed to the heavy taxation of entertainments. It would we well worth while rationing bread moderately in order to bring in the more nourishing Lend-Lease foods. It would be better to ration than to let the stocks run down. Bread is scandalously wasted now and often fed to pigs and chickens. The great thing is to keep the price down, so that the poorest can buy their full ration.

I deprecate the policy of 'Misery first', which is too often inculcated by people who are glad to see war-weariness spread as a prelude to surrender.

The value of all the various self-strafing proposals should be estimated in tonnage of imports. If there is a heavy economy to be achieved with any article, let us effect it; but it would be unwise to embark upon a lot of fussy restrictions in order to give, or try to give, satisfaction to the Fleet Street journalists, who are exempted from military service, have no burden of responsibility to bear, and live in the restaurants of the Strand.

You should draft something for me couched in more decorous form.

The true guide of life is to do what is right.

I do not in the least mind being called a goose. I have been called many worse things than that.

Since the dawn of the Christian era a certain way of life has slowly been shaping itself among the western peoples, and certain standards of conduct and government have come to be esteemed. After many miseries and prolonged confusion, there arose into the broad light of day the conception of the right of the individual; his right to be consulted in the government of his country; his right to invoke the law even against the State itself.

The dawn of 1943 will soon loom red before us, and we must brace ourselves to cope with the trials and problems of what must be a stern and terrible year. We do so with the assurance of ever-growing strength, and we do so as a nation with a strong will, a bold heart and a good conscience.

. . . If we wish to abridge the slaughter and ruin which this war is spreading to so many lands and to which we must ourselves contribute so grievous a measure of suffering and sacrifice, we cannot afford to relax a single fibre of our being or to tolerate the slightest abatement of our efforts. The enemy is still proud and powerful. He is hard to get at. He still possesses enormous armies, vast resources, and invaluable strategic territories. War is full of mysteries and surprises. A false step, a wrong direction, an error in strategy, discord or lassitude among the Allies, might soon give the common enemy power to confront us with new and hideous facts. We have surmounted many serious dangers, but there is one grave danger which will go along with us till the end; that danger is the undue prolongation of the war. No one can tell what new complications and perils might arise in four or five more years of war. And it is in the dragging-out of the war at enormous expense, until the Democracies are tired or bored or split, that the main hopes of Germany and Japan must now reside. We must destroy this hope, as we have destroyed so many others, and for that purpose we must beware of every topic however attractive and every tendency however natural, which turns our minds and energies from this supreme objective of the general victory of the United Nations. By singleness of purpose, by steadfastness of conduct, by tenacity and endurance such as we have so far displayed—by these, and only by these, can we discharge our duty to the future of the world and to the destiny of man.

Speech to U.S. Congress, May 19, 1943

But I am here to tell you that, whatever form your system of world security may take, however the nations are grouped and ranged, whatever derogations are made from national sovereignty for the sake of the large synthesis, nothing will work soundly or for long without the united effort of the British and American peoples.

If we are together nothing is impossible. If we are divided all will fail. I therefore preach continually the doctrine of the fraternal association of our two peoples, not for any purpose of gaining invidious material advantages for either of them, not for territorial aggrandisement or the vain pomp of earthly domination, but for the sake of service to mankind and for the honour that comes to those who faithfully serve great causes.

Here let me say how proud we ought to be, young and old alike, to live in this tremendous, thrilling, formative epoch in the human story, and how fortunate it was for the world that when these great trials came upon it there was a generation that terror could not conquer and brutal violence could not enslave. Let all who are here remember, as the words of the hymn we have just sung suggest, let all of us who are here remember that we are on the stage of history, and that whatever our station may be, and whatever part we have to play, great or small, our conduct is liable to be scrutinized not only by history but by our own descendants.

Let us rise to the full level of our duty and of our opportunity, and let us thank God for the spiritual rewards he has granted for all forms of valiant and faithful service.

Speech at Harvard University, September 6, 1943

It has been said that the price of freedom is eternal vigilance. The question arises, 'What is freedom?' There are one or two quite simple, practical tests by which it can be known in the modern world in peace conditions —namely :

Is there the right to free expression of opinion and of opposition and criticism of the Government of the day?

Have the people the right to turn out a Government of which they disapprove, and are constitutional means provided by which they can make their will apparent?

Are their courts of justice free from violence by the Executive and from threats of mob violence, and free of all association with particular political parties?

Will these courts administer open and well-established laws which are associated in the human mind with the broad principles of decency and justice?

Will there be fair play for poor as well as for rich, for private persons as well as Government officials?

Will the rights of the individual, subject to his duties to the State, be maintained and asserted and exalted?

Is the ordinary peasant or workman who is earning a living by daily toil and striving to bring up a family free from the fear that some grim police organization under the control of a single party, like the Gestapo started by the Nazi and Fascist parties, will tap him on the shoulder and pack him off without fair or open trial to bondage or ill-treatment?

Message to Italian people, August 28, 1944

I have no fear of the future. Let us go forward into its mysteries, let us tear aside the veils which hide it from our eyes, and let us move onward with confidence and courage. All the problems of the post-war world, some of which seem so baffling now, will be easier of solution once decisive victory has been gained, and once it is clear that victory won in arms has not been cast away by folly or by violence when the moment comes to lay the broad foundations of the future world order, and it is time to speak great words of peace and truth to all.

Speech at Royal Albert Hall, September 29, 1943

When Herr Hitler escaped his bomb on July 20 he described his survival as providential; I think that from a purely military point of view we can all agree with him, for certainly it would be most unfortunate if the Allies were to be deprived, in the closing phases of the struggle, of that form of warlike genius by which Corporal Schickelgruber has so notably contributed to our victory.

At this point, I will take a little lubrication, if it is

permissible. I think it is always a great pleasure to the noble Lady the Member for the Sutton Division of Plymouth [Viscountess Astor] to see me drinking water.

House of Commons speech, December 8, 1944

Everyone has his day, and some days last longer than others.

. . . The German war is therefore at an end. After years of intense preparation, Germany hurled herself on Poland at the beginning of September 1939; and, in pursuance of our guarantee to Poland and in agreement with the French Republic, Great Britain, the British Empire and Commonwealth of Nations, declared war upon this foul aggression. After gallant France had been struck down we, from this island and from our united Empire, maintained the struggle single-handed for a whole year until we were joined by the military might of Soviet Russia, and later by the overwhelming power and resources of the United States of America.

Finally almost the whole world was combined against the evil-doers, who are now prostrate before us. Our gratitude to our splendid allies goes forth from all our hearts in this island and throughout the British Empire.

We may allow ourselves a brief period of rejoicing; but let us not forget for a moment the toil and efforts that lie ahead. Japan, with all her treachery and greed, remains unsubdued. The injury she has inflicted on Great Britain, the United States, and other countries, and her detestable cruelties, call for justice and retribution. We must now devote all our strength and resources to the completion of our task, both at home and abroad. Advance, Britannia. Long live the cause of freedom, God save the King.

World broadcast, May 8, 1945

God bless you all. This is your victory! It is the victory of the cause of freedom in every land. In all our long history we have never seen a greater day than this. Everyone, man or woman has done their best. Everyone has tried. Neither the long years, nor the dangers, nor the fierce attacks of the enemy, have in any way weakened the independent resolve of the British nation. God bless you all.

Speech to crowds in Whitehall, May 8, 1945

I wish I could tell you tonight that all our toils and troubles were over. Then indeed I could end my five years' service happily, and if you thought that you had had enough of me and that I ought to be put out to grass, I tell you I would take it with the best of grace. But, on the contrary, I must warn you, as I did when I began this five years' task—and no one knew then that it would last so long—that there is still a lot to do, and that you must be prepared for further efforts of mind and body and further sacrifices to great causes if you are not to fall back into the rut of inertia, the confusion of aim, and the craven fear of being great. You must not weaken in any way in your alert and vigilant frame of mind. Though holiday rejoicing is necessary to the human spirit, yet it must add to the strength and resilience with which every man and woman turns again to the work they have to do, and also to the outlook and watch they have to keep on public affairs.

On the continent of Europe we have yet to make sure that the simple and honourable purposes for which we entered the war are not brushed aside or overlooked in the months following our success, and that the words 'freedom', 'democracy', and 'liberation' are not distorted from their true meaning as we have understood them. There would be little use in punishing the Hitlerites for their crimes if law and justice did not rule, and if totalitarian or police Governments were to take the place of the German invaders. We seek nothing for ourselves. But we must make sure that those causes which we fought for find recognition at the peace table in facts as well as words, and above all we must labour that the world organization which the United Nations are creating at San Francisco does not become an idle name, does not become a shield for the strong and a mockery for the weak. It is the victors who must search their hearts in their glowing hours, and be worthy by their nobility of the immense forces that they wield.

We must never forget that beyond all lurks Japan, harassed and failing but still a people of a hundred millions, for whose warriors death has few terrors. I cannot tell you tonight how much time or what exertions will be required to compel the Japanese to make amends for their odious treachery and cruelty. We—like China, so long undaunted—have received horrible injuries from them ourselves, and we are bound by the ties of honour and fraternal loyalty to the United States to fight this great war at the other end of the world at their side without flagging or failing. We must remember that Australia and New Zealand and Canada were and are all directly menaced by this evil Power. They came to our aid in our dark times, and we must not leave unfinished any task which concerns their safety and their future. I told you hard things at the beginning of these last five years; you did not shrink, and I should be unworthy of your confidence and generosity if I did not still cry : Forward, unflinching, unswerving, indomitable, till the whole task is done and the whole world is safe and clean.

Broadcast, May 13, 1945

The British people are good all through. You can test them as you would put a bucket into the sea, and always find it salt. The genius of our people springs from every class and from every part of the land. You cannot tell where you will not find a wonder. The hero, the fighter, the poet, the master of science, the organizer, the artist, the engineer, the administrator, or the jurist—he may spring into fame. Equal opportunity for all, under free institutions and equal laws—there is the banner for which we will do battle against all rubber-stamp bureaucracies or dictatorships.

Broadcast, June 13, 1945

I do not admit as democratic constitutional doctrine that anything that is stuck into a party manifesto thereupon becomes a mandated right if the electors vote for the party who draw up the manifesto.

Short words are best and the old words when short are best of all.

Writing a book was an adventure. To begin with it was a toy, an amusement; then it became a mistress, and then a master, and then a tyrant.

The reason for having diplomatic relations is not to confer a compliment, but to secure a convenience.

This revelation (the atom bomb) of the secrets of nature, long mercifully withheld from man, should arouse the most solemn reflections in the mind and conscience of every human being capable of comprehension. We must indeed pray that these awful agencies will be made to conduce to peace among the nations, and that instead of wreaking measureless havoc upon the entire globe they may become a perennial fountain of world prosperity.

August 6, 1945

This crowning deliverance (the surrender of Japan) from the long and anxious years of danger and carnage should rightly be celebrated by Parliament in accordance with custom and tradition. The King is the embodiment of the national will, and his public acts involve all the might and power not only of the people of this famous island but of the whole British Commonwealth and Empire. The good cause for which His Majesty has contended commanded the ardent fidelity of all his subjects spread over one-fifth of the surface of the habitable globe. That cause has now been carried to complete success. Total war has ended in absolute victory.

Once again the British Commonwealth and Empire emerges safe, undiminished and united from a mortal struggle. Monstrous tyrannies which menaced our life have been beaten to the ground in ruin, and a brighter radiance illumines the Imperial Crown than any which our annals record. The light is brighter because it comes not only from the fierce but fading glare of military achievement such as an endless succession of conquerors have known, but because there mingle with it in mellow splendour the hopes, joys, and blessings of almost all mankind. This is the true glory, and long will it gleam upon our forward path.

House of Commons, August 15, 1945

. . . I am surprised that in my later life I should have become so experienced in taking degrees, when, as a schoolboy I was so bad at passing examinations. In fact one might almost say that no one ever passed so few examinations and received so many degrees. From this a superficial thinker might argue that the way to get the most degrees is to fail in the most examinations. This would, however, Ladies and Gentlemen, be a conclusion unedifying in the academic atmosphere in which I now preen myself, and I therefore hasten to draw another moral with which I am sure we shall be in accord : namely, that no boy or girl should ever be disheartened by lack of success in their youth but should diligently and faithfully continue to persevere and make up for lost time. There at least is a sentiment which I am sure the Faculty and the Public, the scholars and the dunces will all be cordially united upon.

This raises the interesting question of the age at which knowledge and learning may be most fruitfully imparted and acquired. Owing to the pressure of life and everyone having to earn their living, a University education of the great majority of those who enjoy that high privilege is usually acquired before twenty. These are great years for young people. The world of thought and history and the treasures of learning are laid open to them. They have the chance of broadening their minds, elevating their view and arming their moral convictions by all the resources that free and wealthy communities can bestow. It is the glory of the United States that her graduates of universities are numbered not by the million but by the 10 million, and certainly any young man or woman who has these measureless advantages laid before them and has not the mother wit to profit by them to the full has no right to complain if he or she makes only a mediocre success of life.

Still, Mr. President, I am going to put in a plea for the late starters. Not only is the saying true, 'It is never too late to mend', but university education may be even better appreciated by those in the early twenties than by those in the later teens. The attention which a mature mind can bring to a study of the philosophies, humanities and the great literary monuments of the past is stronger and more intense than at an earlier age. The power of concentration, the retentiveness of the memory, the earnestness and zeal with which conclusions are sought should, in most cases, be greater in the older students. This, Ladies and Gentlemen, has a practical and supreme application at the present time. Millions of young men have had their education interrupted by the war. Their lives have been slashed across by its flaming sword. We must make sure that, in both our countries, they do not suffer needlessly for this particular form of the sacrifice which they have made . . .

. . . This is an age of machinery and specialization but I hope, none the less—indeed all the more—that the purely vocational aspect of university study will not be allowed to dominate or monopolise all the attention of the returned Service men. Engines were made for men, not men for engines. Mr. Gladstone said many years ago that it ought to be part of a man's religion to see that his country is well governed. Knowledge of the past is the only foundation we have from which to peer into and try to measure the future. Expert knowledge, however indispensable, is no substitute for a generous and comprehending outlook upon the human story with all its sadness and with all its unquenchable hope.

May I not also advance the claims of literature and language. The great Bismark—there were great Germans in those days—said at the close of his life, that the most important fact in the world was that the British and American peoples spoke the same language. Certainly we have a noble inheritance in literature. It would be an enormous waste and loss to us all if we did not respect, cherish, enjoy and develop this magnificent estate, which has come down to us from the past and which not only unites us as no such great communities have ever been united before, but is also a powerful instrument whereby our conception of justice, of freedom and of fair play and good humour may make their invaluable contribution to the future progress of mankind.

Speech at Miami University, February 26, 1946

. . . We are the only unbroken nation that fought against Hitler's tyranny in the war from start to finish. We declared war upon Germany when Hitler invaded Poland. We sought no material gains; we coveted no man's land or treasure. We, and with us the whole Empire and Commonwealth, all unprepared as we were, or partly prepared, drew the sword against the mighty antagonist at the call of honour and in defence of the rights of weaker nations, according to our plighted word, according to the fair play of the world. We did not fight only in the sacred cause of self defence, like the Russian patriots who defended their native soil with sublime devotion and glorious success. No one attacked us. We fought for a higher and broader theme. We fought against tyranny, aggression and broken faith, and in order to establish that rule of law among the nations . . .

Speech on receiving the Freedom of Westminster, May 7, 1946

. . . The manpower and much of the physical and moral strength of France was exhausted by the sacrifices she had made for the victory of 1918. The world must never forget that two million Frenchmen gave their lives. With the British Empire it was a million but from a far larger population. The injury inflicted by the First Great War upon the life-energies of France was profound. Crowned with victory, lighted by glory she was drained of blood . . .

Speech at Metz, July 14, 1946

For my part I consider that it will be found much better by all Parties to leave the past to history, especially as I propose to write that history myself.

The right hon. Gentleman will excuse me if I say that he does not seem quite to have got clear of the General Election. A great deal of his speech was made up of very effective points and quips which gave a great deal of satisfaction to those behind him. We all understand his position : 'I am their leader, I must follow them.'

I wish to speak to you today about the tragedy of Europe. This noble continent, comprising on the whole the fairest and the most cultivated regions of the earth, enjoying a temperate and equable climate, is the home of all the great parent races of the western world. It is the fountain of Christian faith and Christian ethics. It is the origin of most of the culture, arts, philosophy and science both of ancient and modern times. If Europe were once united in the sharing of its common inheritance, there would be no limit to the happiness, to the prosperity and glory which its three or four hundred million people would enjoy. Yet it is from Europe that have sprung that series of frightful nationalistic quarrels, originated by the Teutonic nations, which we have seen even in this twentieth century and in our own lifetime, wreck the peace and mar the prospects of all mankind.

And what is the plight to which Europe has been reduced? Some of the smaller States have indeed made a good recovery, but over wide areas a vast quivering mass of tormented, hungry, care-worn and bewildered human beings gape at the ruins of their cities and homes, and scan the dark horizons for the approach of some new peril, tyranny or terror. Among the victors there is a babel of jarring voices; among the vanquished the sullen silence of despair. That is all that Europeans, grouped in so many ancient States and nations, that is all that the Germanic Powers have got by tearing each other to pieces and spreading havoc far and wide. Indeed, but for the fact that the great Republic across the Atlantic Ocean has at length realised that the ruin or enslavement of Europe would involve their own fate as well, and has stretched out hands of succour and guidance, the Dark Ages would have returned in all their cruelty and squalor. They may still return.

Yet all the while there is a remedy which, if it were generally and spontaneously adopted, would as if by a miracle transform the whole scene, and would in a few years make all Europe, or the greater part of it, as free and as happy as Switzerland is to-day. What is this sovereign remedy? It is to re-create the European Family, or as much of it as we can, and provide it with a structure under which it can dwell in peace, in safety and in freedom. We must build a kind of United States of Europe. In this way only will hundreds of millions of toilers be able to regain the simple joys and hopes which make life worth living. The process is simple. All that is needed is the resolve of hundreds of millions of men and women to do right instead of wrong and gain as their reward blessing instead of cursing.

Much work has been done upon this task by the exertions of the Pan-European Union which owes so much to Count Coudenhove-Kalergi and which commanded the services of the famous French patriot and statesman, Aristide Briand. There is also that immense body of doctrine and procedure, which was brought into being amid high hopes after the first world war, as the League of Nations. The League of Nations did not fail because of its principles or conceptions. It failed because these principles were deserted by those States who had brought it into being. It failed because the Governments of those days feared to face the facts, and act while time remained. This disaster must not be repeated. There is therefore much knowledge and material with which to build; and also bitter dear-bought experience.

I was very glad to read in the newspapers two days ago that my friend President Truman had expressed his interest and sympathy with this great design. There is no reason why a regional organization of Europe should in any way conflict with the world organization of the United Nations. On the contrary, I believe that the larger synthesis will only survive if it is founded upon coherent natural groupings. There is already a natural grouping in the Western Hemisphere. We British have our own Commonwealth of Nations. These do not weaken, on the contrary they strengthen, the world organization. They are in fact its main support. And why should there not be a European group which could give a sense of enlarged patriotism and common citizenship to the distracted peoples of this turbulent and mighty continent and why should it not take its rightful place with other great groupings in shaping the destinies of men? In order that this should be accomplished there must be an act of faith in which millions of families speaking many languages must consciously take part.

We all know that the two world wars through which we have passed arose out of the vain passion of a newly-united Germany to play the dominating part in the world. In this last struggle crimes and massacres have been committed for which there is no parallel since the invasions of the Mongols in the fourteenth century

223

and no equal at any time in human history. The guilty must be punished. Germany must be deprived of the power to re-arm and make another aggressive war. But when all this has been done, as it will be done, as it is being done, there must be an end to retribution. There must be what Mr. Gladstone many years ago called 'a blessed act of oblivion'. We must all turn our backs upon the horrors of the past. We must look to the future. We cannot afford to drag forward across the years that are to come the hatreds and revenges which have sprung from the injuries of the past. If Europe is to be saved from infinite misery, and indeed from final doom, there must be an act of faith in the European family and an act of oblivion against all the crimes and follies of the past.

Can the free peoples of Europe rise to the height of these resolves of the soul and instincts of the spirit of man? If they can, the wrongs and injuries which have been inflicted will have been washed away on all sides by the miseries which have been endured. Is there any need for further floods of agony? Is it the only lesson of history that mankind is unteachable? Let there be justice, mercy and freedom. The peoples have only to will it, and all will achieve their hearts' desire.

I am now going to say something that will astonish you. The first step in the re-creation of the European family must be a partnership between France and Germany. In this way only can France recover the moral leadership of Europe. There can be no revival of Europe without a spiritually great France and a spiritually great Germany. The structure of the United States of Europe, if well and truly built, will be such as to make the material strength of a single state less important. Small nations will count as much as large ones and gain their honour by their contribution to the common cause. The ancient states and principalities of Germany, freely joined together for mutual convenience in a federal system, might each take their individual place among the United States of Europe. I shall not try to make a detailed programme for hundreds of millions of people who want to be happy and free, prosperous and safe, who wish to enjoy the four freedoms of which the great President Roosevelt spoke, and live in accordance with the principles embodied in the Atlantic Charter. If this is their wish, they have only to say so, and means can certainly be found, and machinery erected, to carry that wish into full fruition.

But I must give you a warning. Time may be short. At present there is a breathing-space. The cannon have ceased firing. The fighting has stopped; but the dangers have not stopped. If we are to form the United States of Europe or whatever name or form it may take, we must begin now.

In these present days we dwell strangely and precariously under the shield and protection of the atomic bomb. The atomic bomb is still only in the hands of a State and nation which we know will never use it except in the cause of right and freedom. But it may well be that in a few years this awful agency of destruction will be widespread and the catastrophe following from its use by several warring nations will not only bring to an end all that we call civilization, but may possibly disintegrate the globe itself.

I must now sum up the propositions which are before you. Our constant aim must be to build and fortify the strength of U.N.O. Under and within that world concept we must re-create the European family in a regional structure called, it may be, the United States of Europe. The first step is to form a Council of Europe. If at first all the States of Europe are not willing or able to join

225

the Union, we must nevertheless proceed to assemble
and combine those who will and those who can. The
salvation of the common people of every race and of
every land from war or servitude must be established
on solid foundations and must be guarded by the readiness of all men and women to die rather than submit to
tyranny. In all this urgent work, France and Germany
must take the lead together. Great Britain, the British
Commonwealth of Nations, mighty America, and I trust
Soviet Russia—for then indeed all would be well—must
be the friends and sponsors of the new Europe and must
champion its right to live and shine.

Speech at Zurich University, September 19, 1946

That is a curious phrase which has crept in. 'Sifted'
would have been a more natural word, and would avoid
any ambiguity with the word 'concealed'. 'Screened' is
a modern vulgarism.

For some years the tendency of Socialist and left-wing
forces has been to gird at the word 'Empire' and to
espouse the word 'Commonwealth'—because Oliver
Cromwell cut off King Charles's head . . . and also
I suppose, because the word 'Commonwealth' seems to
have in it some association with, or suggestion of, the
abolition of private property and the communal owner-
ship of all forms of wealth. This mood is encouraged by
the race of degenerate intellectuals of whom our island
has produced during several generations an unfailing
succession—these very high intellectual persons who,
when they wake up every morning have looked around
upon the British inheritance, whatever it was, to see
what they could find to demolish, to undermine, or
cast away.

No technical knowledge can out-weigh knowledge of the humanities.

The English never draw a line without blurring it.

There is a good saying to the effect that when a new book appears one should read an old one. As an author I would not recommend too strict an adherence to this saying. But I must admit that I have altered my views about the study of classical literature as I have grown older. At school I never liked it. I entirely failed to respond to the many pressing and sometimes painful exhortations which I received to understand the full charm and precision of the classic languages. But it seems to me that should the classic studies die out in Europe and in the modern world, a unifying influence of importance would disappear.

. . . The United States stands at this time at the pinnacle of world power. It is a solemn moment for the American Democracy. For with primacy in power is also joined an awe-inspiring accountability to the future. If you look around you, you must feel not only the sense of duty done but also you must feel anxiety lest you fall below the level of achievement. Opportunity is here now, clear and shining for both our countries. To reject it or ignore it or fritter it away will bring upon us all the long reproaches of the after-time. It is necessary that constancy of mind, persistency of purpose, and the grand simplicity of decision shall guide and rule the conduct of the English-speaking peoples in peace as they did in war. We must, and I believe we shall, prove ourselves equal to this severe requirement.

When American military men approach some serious situation they are wont to write at the head of their directive the words 'over-all strategic concept'. There is wisdom in this, as it leads to clarity of thought. What then is the over-all strategic concept which we should inscribe today? It is nothing less than the safety and welfare, the freedom and progress, of all the homes and families of all the men and women in all the lands. And here I speak particularly of the myriad cottage or apartment homes where the wage-earner strives amid the accidents and difficulties of life to guard his wife and children from privation and bring the family up in the fear of the Lord, or upon ethical conceptions which often play their potent part.

To give security to these countless homes, they must be shielded from the two giant marauders, war and tyranny. We all know the frightful disturbances in which the ordinary family is plunged when the curse of war swoops down upon the bread-winner and those for whom he works and contrives. The awful ruin of Europe, with all its vanished glories, and of large parts of Asia glares us in the eyes. When the designs of wicked men or the aggressive urge of mighty States dissolve over large areas the frame of civilized society, humble folk are confronted with difficulties with which they cannot cope. For them all is distorted, all is broken, even ground to pulp.

When I stand here this quiet afternoon I shudder to visualize what is actually happening to millions now and what is going to happen in this period when famine stalks the earth. None can compute what has been called 'the unestimated sum of human pain'. Our supreme task and duty is to guard the homes of the common people from the horrors and miseries of another war. We are all agreed on that.

Our American military colleagues, after having proclaimed their 'over-all strategic concept' and computed available resources, always proceed to the next step—namely, the method. Here again there is widespread agreement. A world organization has already been erected for the prime purpose of preventing war. U.N.O., the successor of the League of Nations, with the decisive addition of the United States and all that that means, is already at work. We must make sure that its work is fruitful, that it is a reality and not a sham, that it is a force for action, and not merely a frothing of words, that it is a true temple of peace in which the shields of many nations can some day be hung up, and not merely a cockpit in a Tower of Babel. Before we cast away the solid assurances of national armaments for self-preservation we must be certain that our temple is built not upon shifting sands or quagmires, but upon the rock. Anyone can see with his eyes open that our path will be difficult and also long, but if we persevere together as we did in the two world wars—though not, alas, in the interval between them—I cannot doubt that we shall achieve our common purpose in the end.

I have, however, a definite and practical proposal to make for action. Courts and magistrates may be set up but they cannot function without sheriffs and constables. The United Nations Organization must immediately begin to be equipped with an international armed force. In such a matter we can only go step by step, but we must begin now. I propose that each of the Powers and States should be invited to delegate a certain number of air squadrons to the service of the world organization. These squadrons would be trained and prepared in their own countries but would move around in rotation from one country to another. They would wear the uniform of their own countries but with different badges. They would not be required to act against their own nations, but in other respects they would be directed by the world organization. This might be started on a modest scale and would grow as confidence grew. I wished to see this done after the first world war, and I devoutly trust it may be done forthwith.

It would nevertheless be wrong and imprudent to entrust the secret knowledge or experience of the atomic bomb, which the United States, Great Britain, and Canada now share, to the world organization, while it is still in its infancy. It would be criminal madness to cast it adrift in this still agitated and un-united world. No one in any country has slept less well in their beds because this knowledge and the method and the raw materials to apply it, are at present largely retained in American hands. I do not believe we should all have slept so soundly had the positions been reversed and if some Communist or neo-Fascist State monopolised for the time being these dread agencies. The fear of them alone might easily have been used to enforce totalitarian systems upon the free democratic world, with consequences appalling to human imagination. God has willed that this shall not be and we have at least a breathing space to set our house in order before this peril has to be encountered : and even then if no effort is spared, we should still possess so formidable a superiority as to impose effective deterrents upon its employment, or threat of employment, by others. Ultimately, when the essential brotherhood of man is truly embodied and expressed in a world organization with all the necessary practical safeguards to make it effective, these powders would naturally be confided to that world organization.

Now I come to the second danger of these two marauders which threatens the cottage, the home, and the ordinary people—namely, tyranny. We cannot be blind to the fact that the liberties enjoyed by individual citizens throughout the British Empire are not valid in a considerable number of countries, some of which are very powerful. In these States control is enforced upon the common people by various kinds of all-embracing police governments. The power of the State is exercised without restraint, either by dictators or by compact oligarchies operating through a privileged party and a political police. It is not our duty at this time when difficulties are so numerous to interfere forcibly in the internal affairs of countries which we have not conquered in war. But we must never cease to proclaim in fearless tones the great principles of freedom and the rights of man which are the joint inheritance of the English-speaking world and which through Magna Carta, the Bill of Rights, the Habeas Corpus, trial by jury, and the English common law find their most famous expression in the American Declaration of Independence.

All this means that the people of any country have the right, and should have the power by constitutional action, by free unfettered elections, with secret ballot, to choose or change the character or form of government under which they dwell; that freedom of speech and thought should reign; that courts of justice, independent of the executive, unbiased by any party, should administer laws which have received the broad assent of large majorities or are consecrated by time and custom. Here are the title deeds of freedom which should lie in every cottage home. Here is the message of the British and American peoples to mankind. Let us preach what we practise—let us practise what we preach.

I have now stated the two great dangers which menace the homes of the people : War and Tyranny. I have not yet spoken of poverty and privation which are in many cases the prevailing anxiety. But if the dangers of war and tyranny are removed, there is no doubt that science and co-operation can bring in the next few years to the world, certainly in the next few decades newly taught in the sharpening school of war, an expansion of material well-being beyond anything that has yet occurred in human experience. Now, at this sad and breathless moment, we are plunged in the hunger and distress which are the aftermath of our stupendous struggle; but this will pass and may pass quickly, and there is no reason except human folly or sub-human crime which should deny to all the nations the inauguration and enjoyment of an age of plenty. I have often used words which I learned fifty years ago from a great Irish-American orator, a friend of mine, Mr. Bourke Cockran, 'There is enough for all. The earth is a generous mother; she will provide in plentiful abundance food for all her children if they will but cultivate her soil in justice and in peace.' So far I feel that we are in full agreement.

Now, while still pursuing the method of realizing our overall strategic concept, I come to the crux of what I have travelled here to say. Neither the sure prevention of war, nor the continuous rise of world organization will be gained without what I have called the fraternal association of the English-speaking peoples. This means a special relationship between the British Commonwealth and Empire and the United States. This is no time for generalities, and I will venture to be precise. Fraternal association requires not only the growing friendship and mutual understanding between our two vast but kindred systems of society, but the continuance of the intimate relationship between our military advisers, leading to common study of potential dangers, the similarity of weapons and manuals of instructions, and to the interchange of officers and cadets at technical colleges. It should carry with it the continuance of the present facilities for mutual security by the joint use of all Naval and Air Force bases in the possession of either country all over the world. This would perhaps double the mobility of the American Navy and Air Force. It would greatly expand that of the British Empire Forces and it might well lead, if and as the world calms down, to important financial savings. Already we use together a large number of islands; more may well be entrusted to our joint care in the near future.

The United States has already a Permanent Defence Agreement with the Dominion of Canada, which is so devotedly attached to the British Commonwealth and Empire. This Agreement is more effective than many of those which have often been made under formal alliances. This principle should be extended to all British Commonwealths with full reciprocity. Thus, whatever happens, and thus only, shall we be secure ourselves and able to work together for the high and simple causes that are dear to us and bode no ill to any. Eventually there may come—I feel eventually there will come—the principle of common citizenship, but that we may be content to leave to destiny, whose outstretched arm many of us can already clearly see.

There is however an important question we must ask ourselves. Would a special relationship between the United States and the British Commonwealth be inconsistent with our over-riding loyalties to the World Organization? I reply that, on the contrary, it is probably the only means by which that organization will achieve its full stature and strength. There are already the special United States relations with Canada which I have just mentioned, and there are special relations between the United States and the South American

Republics. We British have our twenty years Treaty of Collaboration and Mutual Assistance with Soviet Russia. I agree with Mr. Bevin, the Foreign Secretary of Great Britain, that it might well be a fifty years Treaty so far as we are concerned. We aim at nothing but mutual assistance and collaboration. The British have an alliance with Portugal unbroken since 1384, and which produced fruitful results at critical moments in the late war. None of these clash with the general interest of a world agreement, or a world organization; on the contrary they help it. 'In my father's house are many mansions.' Special associations between members of the United Nations which have no aggressive point against any other country, which harbour no design incompatible with the Charter of the United Nations, far from being harmful, are beneficial and, as I believe, indispensable.

I spoke earlier of the Temple of Peace. Workmen from all countries must build that temple. If two of the workmen know each other particularly well and are old friends, if their families are inter-mingled, and if they have 'faith in each other's purpose, hope in each other's future and charity towards each other's shortcomings'—to quote some good words I read here the other day—why cannot they work together at the common task as friends and partners? Why cannot they share their tools and thus increase each other's working powers? Indeed they must do so or else the temple may not be built, or, being built, it may collapse, and we shall all be proved again unteachable and have to go and try to learn again for a third time in a school of war, incomparably more rigorous than that from which we have just been released. The dark ages may return, the Stone Age may return on the gleaming wings of science, and what might now shower immeasureable material blessings upon mankind, may even bring about its total destruction. Beware, I say; time may be short. Do not let us take the course of allowing events to drift along until it is too late. If there is to be a fraternal association of the kind I have described, with all the extra strength and security which both our countries can derive from it, let us make sure that that great fact is known to the world, and that it plays its part in steadying and stabilising the foundations of peace. There is the path of wisdom. Prevention is better than cure.

A shadow has fallen upon the scenes so lately lighted by the Allied victory. Nobody knows what Soviet Russia and its Communist international organization intends to do in the immediate future, or what are the limits, if any, to their expansive and proselytising tendences. I have a strong admiration and regard for the valiant Russian people and for my wartime comrade, Marshal Stalin. There is deep sympathy and goodwill in Britain —and I doubt not here also—towards the peoples of all the Russias and a resolve to persevere through many differences and rebuffs in establishing lasting friendships. We understand the Russian need to be secure on her western frontiers by the removal of all possibility of German aggression. We welcome Russia to her rightful place among the leading nations of the world. We welcome her flag upon the seas. Above all, we welcome constant, frequent and growing contacts between the Russian people and our own people on both sides of the Atlantic. It is my duty however, for I am sure you would wish me to state the facts as I see them to you, to place before you certain facts about the present position in Europe.

From Stettin in the Baltic to Trieste in the Adriatic, an iron curtain has descended across the Continent. Behind that line lie all the capitals of the ancient states of Central and Eastern Europe. Warsaw, Berlin, Prague,

Vienna, Budapest, Belgrade, Bucharest and Sofia, all these famous cities and the populations around them lie in what I must call the Soviet sphere, and all are subject in one form or another, not only to Soviet influence but to a very high and, in many cases, increasing measure of control from Moscow. Athens alone—Greece with its immortal glories—is free to decide its future at an election under British, American and French observation. The Russian-dominated Polish Government has been encouraged to make enormous and wrongful inroads upon Germany, and mass expulsions of millions of Germans on a scale grievous and undreamed-of are now taking place. The Communist parties, which were very small in all these Eastern States of Europe, have been raised to pre-eminence and power far beyond their numbers and are seeking everywhere to obtain totalitarian control. Police governments are prevailing in nearly every case, and so far, except in Czechoslovakia, there is no true democracy.

Turkey and Persia are both profoundly alarmed and disturbed at the claims which are being made upon them and at the pressure being exerted by the Moscow Government. An attempt is being made by the Russians in Berlin to build up a quasi-Communist party in their zone of Occupied Germany by showing special favours to groups of left-wing German leaders. At the end of the fighting last June, the American and British Armies withdrew westwards, in accordance with an earlier agreement, to a depth at some points of 150 miles upon a front of nearly four hundred miles, in order to allow our Russian allies to occupy this vast expanse of territory which the Western Democracies had conquered.

If now the Soviet Government tries, by separate action, to build up a pro-Communist Germany in their areas, this will cause new serious difficulties in the

British and American zones, and will give the defeated Germans the power of putting themselves up to auction between the Soviets and the Western Democracies. Whatever conclusions may be drawn from these facts—and facts they are—this is certainly not the Liberated Europe we fought to build up. Nor is it one which contains the essentials of permanent peace.

The safety of the world requires a new unity in Europe, from which no nation should be permanently outcast. It is from the quarrels of the strong parent races in Europe that the world wars we have witnessed or which occurred in former times, have sprung. Twice in our own lifetime we have seen the United States, against their wishes and their traditions, against arguments, the force of which it is impossible not to comprehend, drawn by irresistible forces, into these wars in time to secure the victory of the good cause, but only after frightful slaughter and devastation had occurred. Twice the United States has had to send several millions of its young men across the Atlantic to find the war; but now war can find any nation, wherever it may dwell between dusk and dawn. Surely we should work with conscious purpose for a grand pacification of Europe, within the structure of the United Nations and in accordance with its Charter. That I feel is an open cause of policy of very great importance.

In front of the iron curtain which lies across Europe are other causes for anxiety. In Italy the Communist Party is seriously hampered by having to support the Communist-trained Marshal Tito's claims to former Italian territory at the head of the Adriatic. Nevertheless the future of Italy hangs in the balance. Again one cannot imagine a regenerated Europe without a strong France. All my public life I have worked for a strong France and I never lost faith in her destiny, even in the darkest hours. I will not lose faith now. However, in a great number of countries, far from the Russian frontiers and throughout the world, Communist fifth columns are established and work in complete unity and absolute obedience to the directions they receive from the Communist centre. Except in the British Commonwealth and in the United States where Communism is in its infancy, the Communist parties or fifth columns constitute a growing challenge and peril to Christian civilization. These are sombre facts for anyone to have to recite on the morrow of a victory gained by so much splendid comradeship in arms and in the cause of freedom and democracy; but we should be most unwise not to face them squarely while time remains . . .

. . . I have felt bound to portray the shadow which, alike in the west and in the east, falls upon the world. I was a high minister at the time of the Versailles Treaty and a close friend of Mr. Lloyd-George, who was the head of the British delegation at Versailles. I did not myself agree with many things that were done, but I have a very strong impression in my mind of that situation, and I find it painful to contrast it with that which prevails now. In those days there were high hopes and unbounded confidence that the wars were over, and that the League of Nations would become all-powerful. I do not see or feel that same confidence or even the same hopes in the haggard world at the present time.

On the other hand I repulse the idea that a new war is inevitable; still more that it is imminent. It is because I am sure that our fortunes are still in our own hands and that we hold the power to save the future, that I feel the duty to speak out now that I have the occasion and the opportunity to do so. I do not believe that Soviet Russia desires war. What they desire is the fruits of war and the indefinite expansion of their power and doctrines. But what we have to consider here to-day while time remains, is the permanent prevention of war and the establishment of conditions of freedom and democracy as rapidly as possible in all countries. Our difficulties and dangers will not be removed by closing our eyes to them. They will not be removed by mere waiting to see what happens; nor will they be removed by a policy of appeasement. What is needed is a settlement, and the longer this is delayed, the more difficult it will be and the greater our dangers will become.

From what I have seen of our Russian friends and Allies during the war, I am convinced that there is nothing they admire so much as strength, and there is nothing for which they have less respect than for weakness, especially military weakness. For that reason the old doctrine of a balance of power is unsound. We cannot afford, if we can help it, to work on narrow margins, offering temptations to a trial of strength. If the Western Democracies stand together in strict adherence to the principles of the United Nations Charter, their influence for furthering those principles will be immense and no one is likely to molest them. If, however, they become divided or falter in their duty and if these all-important years are allowed to slip away then indeed catastrophe may overwhelm us all.

Last time I saw it all coming and cried aloud to my own fellow-countrymen and to the world, but no one paid any attention. Up till the year 1933 or even 1935, Germany might have been saved from the awful fate which has overtaken her and we might all have been spared the miseries Hitler let loose upon mankind. There never was a war in all history easier to prevent by timely action than the one which has just desolated such great areas of the globe. It could have been prevented in my belief without the firing of a single shot, and Germany might be powerful, prosperous and honoured to-day; but no one would listen and one by one we were all sucked into the awful whirlpool. We surely must not let that happen again. This can only be achieved by reaching now, in 1946, a good understanding on all points with Russia under the general authority of the United Nations Organization and by the maintenance of that good understanding through many peaceful years, by the world instrument, supported by the whole strength of the English-speaking world and all its connections. There is the solution which I respectfully offer to you in this Address to which I have given the title 'The Sinews of Peace'.

Let no man underrate the abiding power of the British Empire and Commonwealth. Because you see the 46 millions in our island harrassed about their food supply, of which they only grow one half, even in wartime, or because we have difficulty in restarting our industries and export trade after six years of passionate war effort, do not suppose that we shall not come through these dark years of privation as we have come through the glorious years of agony, or that half a century from now, you will not see 70 or 80 millions of Britons spread about the world and united in defence of our traditions, our way of life, and of the world causes which you and we espouse. If the population of the English-speaking Commonwealths be added to that of the United States with all that such co-operation implies in the air, on the sea, all over the globe and in science and in industry, and in moral force, there will be no quivering, precarious balance of power to offer its temptation to ambition or adventure. On the contrary, there will be an overwhelming assurance of security. If we adhere faithfully to the Charter of the

United Nations and walk forward in sedate and sober strength seeking no one's land or treasure, seeking to lay no arbitrary control upon the thoughts of men; if all British moral and material forces and convictions are joined with your own in fraternal association, the high-roads of the future will be clear, not only for us but for all, not only for our time, but for a century to come.

Speech at Westminster College, Fulton, Missouri, March 5, 1946

Before I examine that project in detail, there are some general propositions now in vogue which deserve scrutiny. Let me state them in terms of precision : 'All oppression from the Left is progress. All resistance from the Right is reactionary. All forward steps are good, and all backward steps are bad. When you are getting into a horrible quagmire, the only remedy is to plunge in deeper and deeper.' These rules, it seems to me, from time to time require review by the intelligentsia. They require review in the light of experience and of the circumstances we see around us.

The word 'disinflation' has been coined in order to avoid the unpopular term 'deflation'. . . . I suppose that presently when 'disinflation' also wins its bad name, the Chancellor (Sir Stafford Cripps) will call it 'nonundisinflation' and will start again.

It always looks so easy to solve problems by taking the line of least resistance. Again and again in my life I have seen this course lead to the most unexpected result, and what looks like being the easy road turns out to be the hardest and most cruel. No nation is so remarkable as ours for the different moods through which it passes, moments of great dejection, moments of sublime triumph, heroism, fortitude and then exhaustion. What has been gained with enormous effort and sacrifice, prodigious and superb acts of valour, slips away almost unnoticed when the struggle is over.

It excites world wonder in the Parliamentary countries that we should build a Chamber, starting afresh, which can only seat two-thirds of its Members. It is difficult to explain this to those who do not know our ways. They cannot easily be made to understand why we consider that the intensity, passion, intimacy, informality and spontaneity of our Debates constitute the personality of the House of Commons and endow it at once with its focus and its strength. . . . It is the champion of the people against executive oppression . . . the House of Commons has ever been the controller and, if need be, the changer of the rulers of the day and of the Ministers appointed by the Crown. It stands for ever against oligarchy and one-man power. . . . The House of Commons stands for freedom and law, and this is the message which the Mother of Parliaments has proved herself capable of proclaiming to the world at large.

It is with deep grief I watch the clattering down of the British Empire with all its glories, and all the services it has rendered to mankind. I am sure that in the hour of our victory now not so long ago, we had the power to make a solution of our difficulties which would have been honourable and lasting. Many have defended Britain against her foes. None can defend her against herself. We must face the evils that are coming upon us and that we are powerless to avert. We must do our best in all these circumstances and not exclude any expedient that may help to mitigate the ruin and disaster that will follow the disappearance of Britain from the East. But at least, let us not add—by shameful flight, by a premature hurried scuttle—at least, let us not add to the pangs of sorrow so many of us feel, the taint and smear of shame.

House of Commons, March 6, 1947

In this Debate we have had the usual jargon about 'the infrastructure of a supra national authority'. The original authorship is obscure; but it may well be that these words 'infra' and 'supra' have been introduced into our current political parlance by the band of intellectual highbrows who are naturally anxious to impress British labour with the fact that they learned Latin at Winchester.

Young people at universities study to achieve knowledge and not to learn a trade. We must all learn how to support ourselves, but we must also learn how to live. We need a lot of engineers in the modern world, but we do not want a world of modern engineers.

How does the right hon. Gentleman conceive democracy? Just let me explain it to him, Mr. Speaker, or explain some of the more rudimentary elements of it to him. Democracy is not a caucus, obtaining a fixed term of office by promises, and then doing what it likes with the people. We hold that there ought to be a constant relationship between the rulers and the people. Government of the people, by the people, for the people, still remains the sovereign definition of democracy. There is no correspondence between this broad conception and the outlook of His Majesty's Government. Democracy, I must explain to the Lord President, does not mean, 'We have got our majority, never mind how,

243

and we have our lease of office for five years, so what are you going to do about it?' That is not democracy, that is only small party patter, which will not go down with the mass of the people of this country . . .

. . . The whole history of this country shows a British instinct—and, I think I may say, a genius—for the division of power. The American Constitution, with its checks and counterchecks, combined with its frequent appeals to the people, embodies much of the ancient wisdom of this island. Of course, there must be proper executive power to any Government, but our British, our English idea, in a special sense, has always been a system of balanced rights and divided authority, with many other persons and organized bodies having to be considered besides the Government of the day and the officials they employ. This essential British wisdom is expressed in many foreign Constitutions which followed our Parliamentary system, outside the totalitarian zone, but never was it so necessary as in a country which has no written Constitution.

The right hon. Gentlemen spoke about Parliament, about the rights of Parliament, which I shall certainly not fail to defend. But it is not Parliament that should rule; it is the people who should rule through Parliament.

House of Commons, November 11, 1947

But I must tell you that the more kindness and appreciation I meet, the more humble I become. I do not take all this to myself. I know very well how vain it is for individuals to try to gather to themselves the credit which really belongs to the great countries and the great nations whose virtues they have had the opportunity of crediting to themselves in world history. I have often been praised for things I said at the beginning of the War, when England was fighting alone. That was only expressions of my people, it was their courage and great qualities I put into words. And it was what my colleagues wanted me to say—if I had not, they would have pulled me to pieces, as I certainly would have pulled them to pieces the other way round.

I never remember a General Election which was not followed by a disagreeable, sterile, bickering over election pledges.

The bond of discipline is subtle and sensitive. It may be as tense as steel or as brittle as glass. The main element of discipline in the British Service is a sense of justice and a sense of willing association among great bodies of men with the general policy of their country.

The Prime Minister said—and said quite truly—that the House of Commons was the workshop of democracy. But it has other claims, too. It is the champion of the people against executive oppression. I am not making a party point; that is quite unfitting on such an occasion. But the House of Commons has ever been the controller and, if need be, the changer of the rulers of the day and of the Ministers appointed by the Crown. It stands forever against oligarchy and one-man power. All these traditions, which have brought us into being over hundreds of years, carrying a large proportion of the commanding thought of the human race with us, all these traditions received new draughts of life as the franchise was extended until it became universal. The House of Commons stands for freedom and law, and this is the message which the Mother of Parliament has proved herself capable of proclaiming to the world at large . . .

House of Commons, October 24, 1950

245

Man in this moment of his history has emerged in greater supremacy over the forces of nature than has ever been dreamed of before. He has it in his power to solve quite easily the problems of material existence. He has conquered the wild beasts, and he has even conquered the insects and the microbes. There lies before him, as he wishes, a golden age of peace and progress. All is in his hand. He has only to conquer his last and worst enemy—himself. With vision, faith and courage, it may still be within our power to win a crowning victory for all.

House of Commons, March 28, 1950

We have suffered a serious loss in the departure of Mr. Bevin from the Foreign Office. After nearly eleven years of continuous service of the most arduous character it was felt that for some time past he was breaking under the strain. Although I differed from him in his handling of many questions, I feel bound to put on record that he takes his place among the great Foreign Secretaries of our country, and that, in his steadfast resistance to Communist aggression, in his strengthening of our ties with the United States and in his share of building up the Atlantic Pact, he has rendered services to Britain and to the cause of peace which will long be remembered. As his war-time leader I take this opportunity to pay my tribute to him and to his devoted wife.

Broadcast, March 17, 1951

The dominant forces in human history have come from the perception of great truths and the faithful pursuance of great causes.

Moralists may find it a melancholy thought that peace can find no nobler foundation than mutual terror. . . . What is our goal? What is our hearts' wish? It

is very plain, it is very simple. It is only the hearts'
desire of all the millions of ordinary men and women
with their hard workaday lives, all the peoples still outside the totalitarian curtain all over the world—only
their hearts' desire : freedom and peace. The right to be
let alone to lead our own lives in our own way, under
our own laws, and give our children a fair chance to
make the best of themselves. It is not wrong for anyone
to ask for that. It is not much for Britain to ask. We did
our best to fight for it, in the late war; for a whole year
we fought alone. When at last all our enemies surrendered we thought we had won it—won at least for a
lifetime. But now it seems that we are again in jeopardy.
We are in a sad, sombre period of world history where
no good-hearted, valiant Russian soldier, worker or
peasant; no hard-pressed, disillusioned German family;
no home in the war-scarred democracies of Western
Europe or in our own islands we have guarded so long,
so well, or far across the Atlantic in mighty America—
no household can have the feeling after a long day's
faithful toil that they can go to sleep without the fear
that something awful is moving towards them; and this
is what has come to us after all our efforts and sacrifices,
and come upon us at a time when, but for the thought-
lessness of the free democracies and the organized
designs of the Kremlin oligarchy, expanding science,
like a fairy godmother, could have opened the gates of
the Golden Age to all . . .

Broadcast, March 17, 1951

But what I cannot understand is how any of the
leaders of Soviet Russia or the United States or here in
Britain or France or in United Europe or anywhere
else, could possibly imagine that their interests could
be bettered by having an unlimited series of frightful

immeasurable explosions. For another world war would not be like the Crusades or the romantic struggles in former centuries we have read about. It would be nothing less than a massacre of human beings whether in uniform or out of uniform by the hideous forces of perverted science. Science, which now offers us a Golden Age with one hand, offers at the same time with the other hand the doom of all that we have built up inch by inch since the Stone Age.

My faith is in the high progressive destiny of man. I do not believe we are to be flung back into abysmal darkness by those fearsome discoveries which human genius has made. Let us make sure that they are our servants but not our masters. Let us hold fast to the three supreme purposes. The freedom of the individual man in an ordered society; a world organization to prevent bloody quarrels between nations by the rule of law; and for ourselves who have played so great a part in what I have called 'our finest hour', to keep our own fifty millions alive in a small island at the high level of progressive civilization which they have attained. Those are the three goals. To reach them we have first to regain our independence financially, economically and morally. If we are to play our part in the greater affairs of the free world, we have to gather around us our Empire and the States of the British Commonwealth, and bind them ever more closely together. We have to give our hand generously, wholeheartedly, to our Allies across the Atlantic Ocean, upon whose strength and wisdom the salvation of the world at this moment may well depend. Joined with them in fraternal association, drawn and held together by our common language and our joint inheritance of literature and custom, we may save ourselves and save the world.

Election address, October 23, 1951

It is my belief that by accumulating deterrents of all kinds against aggression we shall, in fact, ward off the fearful catastrophe, the fears of which darken the life and mar the progress of all the people of the globe. We must persevere steadfastly and faithfully in the task to which, under the United States leadership, we have solemnly bound ourselves. Any weakening of our purpose, any disruption of our organization would bring about the very evils which we all dread, and from which we should all suffer, and from which many of us would perish.

We must not lose patience, and we must not lose hope. It may be that presently a new mood will reign behind the Iron Curtain. If so it will be easy for them to show it, but the democracies must be on their guard against being deceived by a false dawn. We seek or covet no one's territory; we plan no forestalling war; we trust and pray that all will come right. Even during these years of what is called the 'cold war', material production in every land is continually improving through the use of new machinery and better organization and the advance of peaceful science. But the great bound forward in progress and prosperity for which mankind is longing cannot come till the shadow of war has passed away. There are, however, historic compensations for the stresses which we suffer in the 'cold war'. Under the pressure and menace of Communist aggression the fraternal association of the United States with Britain and the British Commonwealth, and the new unity growing up in Europe—nowhere more hopeful than between France and Germany—all these harmonies are being brought forward, perhaps by several generations in the destiny of the world. If this proves true—and it has certainly proved true up to date—the architects in the Kremlin may be found to have built a different and a far better world structure than what they planned.

Members of the Congress, I have dwelt today repeatedly upon many of the changes that have happened throughout the world since you last invited me to address you here and I am sure you will agree that it is hardly possible to recognize the scene or believe it can truly have come to pass. But there is one thing which is exactly the same as when I was here last. Britain and the United States are working together and working for the same high cause. Bismarck once said that the supreme fact of the nineteenth century was that Britain and the United States spoke the same language. Let us make sure that the supreme fact of the twentieth century is that they tread the same path.

Speech to U.S. Congress, January 17, 1952

My friends, when the death of the King was announced to us yesterday morning there struck a deep and solemn note in our lives which, as it resounded far and wide, stilled the clatter and traffic of twentieth-century life in many lands and made countless millions of human beings pause and look around them. A new sense of values took, for the time being, possession of human minds and mortal existence presented itself to so many at the same moment in its serenity and in its sorrow, in its splendour and in its pain, in its fortitude and in its suffering.

The King was greatly loved by all his peoples. He was respected as a man and as a prince far beyond the many realms over which he reigned. The simple dignity of his life, his manly virtues, his sense of duty alike as a ruler and a servant of the vast spheres and communities for which he bore responsibility—his gay charm and happy nature, his example as a husband and a father in his own family circle, his courage in peace or war—all these were aspects of his character which won the glint of admiration, now here, now there, from the innumerable eyes whose gaze falls upon the Throne.

We thought of him as a young naval lieutenant in the great Battle of Jutland. We thought of him, when calmly, without ambition, or want of self-confidence, he assumed the heavy burden of the Crown and succeeded his brother, whom he loved, and to whom he had rendered perfect loyalty. We thought of him so faithful in his study and discharge of State affairs, so strong in his devotion to the enduring honour of our country, so self-restrained in his judgments of men and affairs, so uplifted above the clash of party politics, yet so attentive to them; so wise and shrewd in his judging between what matters and what does not. All this we saw and admired. His conduct on the Throne may well be a model and a guide to constitutional sovereigns throughout the world today, and also in future generations.

The last few months of King George's life, with all the pain and physical stresses that he endured—his life hanging by a thread from day to day—and he all the time cheerful and undaunted—stricken in body but quite undisturbed and even unaffected in spirit—these have made a profound and an enduring impression and should be a help to all. He was sustained not only by his natural buoyancy but by the sincerity of his Christian faith. During these last months the King walked with death, as if death were a companion, an acquaintance, whom he recognized and did not fear. In the end death came as a friend; and after a happy day of sunshine and sport, and after 'good night' to those who loved him best, he fell asleep as every man or woman who strives to fear God and nothing else in the world may hope to do.

The nearer one stood to him the more these facts were apparent. But the newspapers and photographs of modern times have made vast numbers of his subjects able to watch with emotion the last months of his pilgrimage. We all saw him approach his journey's end. In this period of mourning and meditation, amid our cares and toils, every home in all the realms joined together under the Crown, may draw comfort for tonight and strength for the future from his bearing and his fortitude.

There was another tie between King George and his people. It was not only sorrow and affliction that they shared. Dear to the hearts and the homes of the people is the joy and pride of a united family; with this all the troubles of the world can be borne and all its ordeals at least confronted. No family in these tumultuous years was happier, or loved one another more, than the Royal Family around the King.

My friends, I suppose no Minister saw so much of the King during the war as I did. I made certain he was kept informed of every secret matter; and the care and thoroughness with which he mastered the immense daily flow of State papers made a deep mark on my mind. Let me tell you another fact. On one of the days, when Buckingham Palace was bombed, the King had just returned from Windsor. One side of the courtyard was struck, and if the windows opposite out of which he and the Queen were looking had not been, by the mercy of God, open, they would both have been blinded by the broken glass instead of being only hurled back by the explosion. Amid all that was then going on— although I saw the King so often—I never heard of this episode till a long time after. Their Majesties never mentioned it, or thought it of more significance than a soldier in their armies would of a shell bursting near him. This seems to me to be a revealing trait in the Royal character.

There is no doubt that of all the institutions which have grown up among us over the centuries, or sprung into being in our lifetime, the constitutional monarchy is the most deeply founded and dearly cherished by the whole association of our peoples. In the present generation it has acquired a meaning incomparably more powerful than anyone had dreamed possible in former times. The Crown has become the mysterious link—indeed, I may say, the magic link—which unites our loosely bound but strongly interwoven Commonwealth of nations, States and races. Peoples who would never tolerate the assertions of a written constitution which implied any diminution of their independence, are the foremost to be proud of their loyalty to the Crown.

We have been greatly blessed amid our many anxieties and in the mighty world that has grown up all around our small island—we have been greatly blessed that this new intangible, inexpressible but for practical purposes apparently, an all-powerful element of union should have leapt into being among us. How vital it is, not only to the future of the British Commonwealth and Empire, but I believe also to the cause of world freedom and peace which we serve, that the occupant of the Throne should be equal to the august and indefinable responsibilities which this supreme office requires. For fifteen years King George VI was king; never at any moment in all the perplexities at home and abroad, in public or in private, did he fail in his duties; well does he deserve the farewell salute of all his governments and peoples.

My friends, it is at this time that our compassion and sympathy go out to his Consort and widow. Their marriage was a love match with no idea of regal pomp or splendour. Indeed, there seemed to lie before them the arduous life of royal personages denied so many of the activities of ordinary folk and having to give so much in ceremonial public service. May I say, speaking with all freedom, that our hearts go out tonight to that valiant woman with famous blood of Scotland in her veins who sustained King George through all his toils and problems and brought up, with their charm and beauty, the two daughters who mourn their father today. May she be granted strength to bear her sorrow. To Queen Mary, his mother, another of whose sons is dead—the Duke of Kent having been killed on active service—there belongs the consolation of seeing how well the King did his duty and fulfilled her hopes, and of always knowing how much he cared for her.

Now I must leave the treasures of the past and turn to the future. Famous have been the reigns of our Queens. Some of the greatest periods in our history have unfolded under their sceptres. Now that we have the Second Queen Elizabeth, also ascending the Throne in her twenty-sixth year, our thoughts are carried back nearly 400 years to the magnificent figure who presided over, and in many ways embodied and inspired, the grandeur and genius of the Elizabethan Age. Queen Elizabeth the Second, like her predecessor, did not pass her childhood in any certain expectation of the Crown. But already we know her well, and we understand why her gifts and those of her husband, the Duke of Edinburgh, have stirred the only part of our Commonwealth she has yet been able to visit. She has already been acclaimed as Queen of Canada : we make our claim too, and others will come forward also; and tomorrow the proclamation of her sovereignty will command the loyalty of her native land and of all other parts of the British Commonwealth and Empire.

I, whose youth was passed in the august, unchallenged and tranquil glories of the Victorian Era, may well feel a thrill in invoking, once more, the prayer and the Anthem

GOD SAVE THE QUEEN

Broadcast, February 7, 1952

A fair and youthful figure, Princess, wife and mother, is the heir to all our traditions and glories never greater than in her father's days, and to all our perplexities and dangers never greater in peacetime than now. She is also heir to all our united strength and loyalty. She comes to the Throne at a time when a tormented mankind stands uncertainly poised between world catastrophe and a golden age. That it should be a golden age of art and letters, we can only hope—science and machinery have their other tales to tell—but it is certain that if a true and lasting peace can be achieved, and if the nations will only let each other alone an immense and undreamed of prosperity with culture and leisure ever more widely spread can come, perhaps even easily and swiftly, to the masses of the people in every land. Let us hope and pray that the accession to our ancient Throne of Queen Elizabeth the Second may be the signal for such a brightening salvation of the human scene.

House of Commons, February 11, 1952

Nothing can save England if she will not save herself. If we lose faith in ourselves, in our capacity to guide and govern, if we lose our will to live, then indeed our story is ended.

Armoury House, London, April 23, 1953

TANDEM BOOKS

The publishers hope that you enjoyed this book and invite you to write for their list of other titles which is available free of charge.

UNIVERSAL-TANDEM PUBLISHING CO. LTD.

33 BEAUCHAMP PLACE
LONDON SW3